SOMETHING EXT

Something Extraordinary is Happening

The Sunderland Experience
of the Holy Spirit

ANDY AND JANE FITZ-GIBBON

MONARCH
Crowborough

First published 1995

Unless otherwise indicated, biblical quotations are from
the New Revised Standard Version, 1989.

British Library Cataloguing-in-Publication Data.
A catalogue record for this book is available
from the British Library.

ISBN 1 85424 329 2

Designed and produced by
Bookprint Creative Services
P. O. Box 827, BN21 3YJ, England for
MONARCH PUBLICATIONS
Broadway House, The Broadway
Crowborough, E. Sussex, TN6 1HQ.
Printed in Great Britain.

To Ken and Lois
whose openness to God,
courage and faithfulness
facilitated the renewal at Sunderland

and

to all who have drunk deeply at the well
and who have generously
shared their stories with us

CONTENTS

FOREWORD

It is indeed my pleasure to introduce Andy and Jane Fitz-Gibbon's book telling the story of God at work in Sunderland, England. Little did I realise, when I first met Ken and Lois Gott in Toronto in August of 1994, what great things God had in store for them and their church.

Being in Sunderland in April 1995 was a wonderful and particular joy for Carol and myself. This was our second visit to the North-east and how thrilling it was to see this part of England on fire for God and well attended by visitors from all over the British Isles, Ireland and several other European countries. They came to be bathed in the love of God and it was exciting to see long-standing desires for 'more of him' being realised. The church is being impregnated with life and excitement such as has not been witnessed in decades. Ancient Celtic Christian fervor has been reactivated as the well of God's blessing has been redug in the country. Men and women from every denomination, as well as many nations, are receiving healing for both body and soul. To God be the glory!

Carol and I are particulary thrilled to have had some input into this amazing story at the Sunderland Christian Centre with Ken and Lois Gott. These are two very precious and godly people. We now count them among our dearest friends. They have a great love for one

9

another and for the kingdom of God, which I'm sure is a
centrepiece in the work of grace that God is doing there.
Ken and Lois are two of the nicest and most humble, yet
dedicated servants of the Lord that I have ever met and
we are delighted about the Toronto/Sunderland connection.

It was our pleasure also to meet Andy and Jane Fitz-
Gibbon in October of 1994 when we were first there
visiting the area. This exciting book on the Sunderland
experience with the Holy Spirit reflects scholarly insights
and evaluations, tempered with both personal and eye-
witness accounts from Andy and Jane. I am honoured to
endorse this work which tells the wonderful, continuing
story of the acts of the Holy Spirit.

May you, dear reader, receive light and understanding
as you read through this volume. May your own heart be
warmed and filled, and may your understand be enlight-
ened as you enjoy the 'Sunderland Blessing', so honestly
presented here. As the fires of renewal and revival
continue both to spread and intensify, I expect that this
book will take its place as a helpful tool to equip and
inform the 'hungry-after-God'.

'May the earth be filled with the knowledge of the
glory of the Lord as the waters cover the sea' (Habakkuk
3:14).

John Arnott, Senior Pastor
Toronto Airport Vineyard

PROLOGUE

God must have a sense of humour! Ken Gott opened his eyes to see, to his amazement, a baptismal font towering above his head.

All his life Ken had believed that the Pentecostal churches had a monopoly on the Holy Spirit. When a wave of the Spirit reached the British Isles in the early 1980s through John Wimber's teaching and visits, Ken had resolutely stood apart from it. Somehow, the renewal which had reached many other Christian denominations did not have the same authentic ring to it as had been true of 'Classic Pentecostalism'.

Yet, here in an Anglican church in Knightsbridge, beneath a font, God was pouring the Holy Spirit into Ken's life in a way he had never experienced before. With the comic irony of his position Ken simply laughed and laughed, not merely as if chuckling at a funny story, but the deep, convulsive, releasing laughter that many Christians had begun to experience. Ken Gott laughed that day for a solid hour-and-a-half. This was the beginning of an amazing move of God in the North-East of England which continues at the time of writing, some eight months down the road.

The story of the 'Toronto Blessing' has been told well in

other places.[1] By August 1994 many churches in England had experienced holy laughter, shaking, groaning, falling and other phenomena often associated with periods of revival. It had not as yet, apart from a few isolated incidences, reached the North-East. It's one of the common complaints of north-easterners that southerners always have priority! In the daily weather forecasts the South-East is always mentioned first, not surprisingly, of course, with the nation's capital and its heart of commerce and government. Nonetheless, there is still sometimes a feeling of being marginalised, even forgotten in the North-East.

However, just as surely as the weather forecaster eventually mentions the North, so too religious trends find their way northwards. In terms of the current move of God's Spirit we have drunk deeply as God has seen fit to redig a well where saints have drunk in past centuries.

There had been rumours, of course. Not only denominational papers and the Christian press, but the national media had covered stories about the new phenomena as either 'mass hysteria' or 'revival' happening in London. When Ken Gott's good friend Wes Richards, a pastor from Slough, invited him to a meeting at Holy Trinity, Brompton—complete with plane ticket—Ken simply had to go.

So it was, in a setting culturally alien, and a long way from his beloved North-East roots, Ken entered the 'refreshing'. The dynamic juxtaposition of Pentecostal meeting Anglican (and many other denominations) became symbolic of all that God was going to do in the following months in northern England. Great dividing walls were about to come down. Denominationalism would become an irrelevance for many. Broken relationships would be restored, new friendships formed and an

---

[1] See Appendix

amazing unity achieved *without human effort or planning* as God poured out his Spirit on all flesh.

On reflection Ken comments, 'The truth is we were there because we were dry, spiritually bankrupt and barren. We were also desperate. The bottom line was we needed God'.[2] It was a humbling experience for five Pentecostal leaders to approach a bishop of the established church for prayer to receive the Holy Spirit. Even David Pytches' prayer was somewhat 'unpentecostal'. In a quiet and undemonstrative way he merely asked God to bless 'these dear men'. God answered the prayer as all five fell to the ground virtually instantaneously.

The whole experience marked a dramatic change for Ken Gott. Throughout his whole ministry he had sought to model himself on some of the world's greatest and most anointed 'platform ministries'—ministries in which the pattern is where those on the platform demonstrate great spiritual anointing and prayer is offered by them for the gathered people (sometimes in their thousands). The shift for Ken was that the ministry was to be taken from the platform and given to the whole body of Christ.

God spoke clearly to Ken 'I want my church back!' With amazing humility Ken along with his wife Lois, with whom Ken shares the ministry at Sunderland Christian Centre (SCC), obeyed God. Their faithful obedience resulted in a church set free and a truly astounding release of the ministry and gifting of the whole church. Ken comments, 'I was committed to trusting the work of the Holy Spirit in a person's life and trusting the hearts of the people'.

One of the remarkable and visible aspects of the Sunderland renewal is the very clear 'hands-off' approach of the leadership. From the beginning the renewal was

---

[2] From Ken's testimony in *Times of Refreshing*, no. 1, January 1995, the newsletter of the Sunderland renewal.

seen to be a work of God, even a holy thing. To 'touch the ark' would be perhaps to lose the blessing. As the renewal has progressed Ken and Lois Gott have 'given away' the ministry allowing many to flow in God's power. Ministry teams are led and composed of people from many churches encompassing virtually all the denominations, as are the worship leaders and musicians. Preachers, likewise, have been many and varied, both 'lay' and 'ordained'. No one has sought to 'own' or 'possess' the renewal. It seems to please God, as blessing is poured out night after night with great beauty and power.

The place of God's visitation

Sunderland Christian Centre began eight years previously as a plant from the Bethshan Christian Centre in Newcastle-upon-Tyne, both churches being Assembly of God. Growth had been steady and God had been good to the new church. In 1992, through the sacrificial giving of many members (some even sold houses and bought smaller ones) a new building was opened in the East End of Sunderland, close to the docks.

The Hendon district of Sunderland is not one of the city's more prosperous parts. Sadly, crime is rampant. Sunderland has the dubious honour of being the European Community's black spot for car theft. In forced recognition of this reality SCC is situated within a compound, surrounded by an eight foot high security fence and all the glass in the building is brick-proof polycarbonate. Cars parked within the 'compound' are given some security: during the renewal meetings between three and six security guards are employed each night. Outside the compound any vehicle left unattended is fair game for petty criminals. The compound is full every night, with cars sometimes parked four abreast.

Into a building in such unlikely surroundings thousands of people, from all over Britain and parts of Europe and beyond, have flocked night after night.

When Ken arrived back from his brief trip to London the congregation noticed an immediate change. They were so impressed that they decided to send Ken, Lois and the church's youth pastor to Toronto to experience the refreshing at first hand. Ken reports that they soaked in God for a week, found their spiritual passion restored and returned home renewed.

On August 14th, the first Sunday morning back from Toronto, the effect on the church was staggering. Virtually the whole congregation responded to Ken's appeal to receive the same touch from God that he and Lois had received. They decided to meet again in the evening, although normal meetings had been postponed for the summer recess. The same experience occurred. They gathered again the next evening and the next . . . in fact for two weeks without a night off. Quickly, numbers grew from around a hundred-and-fifty to six hundred. Word reached the region and, without advertising, people began the pilgrimage to Sunderland from a radius of around 70 miles.

By September a pattern of nightly meetings (bar Mondays) was established and each night the same overwhelming sense of God was present. That pattern has continued ever since, with a monthly leaders' meeting on a Wednesday or Thursday afternoon (with usually round 300 in attendance) and a daily 'place' of prayer being added.

The effect on many churches and on thousands of individuals has been profound. Indeed, we are very much aware that in telling the story we are only beginning to scratch the surface of the immensity of the move of God centred on Sunderland. Literally thousands have been touched for the better.

Bathed in such love

Ken and Lois Gott make a remarkable team. We have always noticed a special anointing whenever they are ministering together. We wondered how what was happening in Sunderland had affected Lois. She told us a little of her story,

'One fine sunshine filled day in June [1994] Ken and I sat sunning ourselves in our garden. However, the beauty of the day couldn't lift our spirits. We belonged to what appeared to be a successful, growing church, seeing souls saved weekly and the church numerically growing very satisfactorily.

'Despite this, the burden upon my husband and myself was considerable. We were stretched too far, we were burnt out, the ministry was a performance rather than a service, we felt pressured and more than a little stressed out.' It was then that the telephone rang and Ken was invited to visit Holy Trinity Brompton.

Lois was a little puzzled by the phone call she received from Ken, in London, the next day. He just laughed hysterically! However Lois saw the difference on his return.

'I knew he had most definitely had an encounter with the Lord. He had a passion for Jesus burning in him I hadn't seen for a long time and a desire to be totally obedient to the Father.'

Lois was convinced that the change in Ken was of God but admits to a slight reserve concerning the manifestations. It was in this frame of mind that she visited the Airport Vineyard in Toronto. The first meeting was something of a surprise due to the casual style of the Vineyard team compared to the more formal Pentecostal tradition. She says,

'The first "spiritual culture shock" for me was seeing the singers and musicians in casual clothing, wearing baseball caps and many sporting long hair! Nowhere did I see a suit. This truly was a different world. As the evening progressed I grew more and more amazed at the extreme manifestations I was witnessing.'

For Lois her personal encounter with the Holy Spirit, a life changing experience, came on the Sunday morning: 'The Holy Spirit bathed me in such love that a great inner healing took place. Eight years previously we had lost our only son at birth. The whole experience of haemorrhage and shock had left me with a secret but serious fear of death, doctors and hospitals.

'While I lay on the floor of that inauspicious place I had, to my utter astonishment, a vision of heaven. At that very moment such joy, peace and love diffused my whole being. I wept and wept as I wondered over and over again why I had been so afraid and wasted so much time in fear. For eight years I had lived in bondage and fear and in a few moments I was released to peace and joy. My love for my Saviour welled up in a physical ache for the One who died that I might live. Not only did I receive a deep inner healing that morning, but a profound love for the Lord Jesus Christ that has motivated me each day for the last nine months.'

A record of grace

Luke said at the beginning of his gospel:

> Since many have undertaken to set down an orderly account of the events that have been fulfilled among us, just as they were handed on to us by those who from the beginning were eyewitnesses and servants of the word, I too decided, after investigating everything carefully from the very first, to write an orderly account for you, most excellent Theophilus, so that you may know the truth concerning the things about which you have been instructed.
>
> Luke 1:1–4

We find ourselves in something of the same position. We have been sharing in the renewal at Sunderland now for eight months at least three nights a week. We have seen between two and seven hundred gather nightly to be refreshed by God. We have had the privilege of listening to numerous testimonies to God's goodness as, normally, each night between six and ten people testify of what God has done in their lives. We have heard stories of how people have fallen in love with Jesus again, how relationships between individuals and between churches have been healed, we've heard of physical healings and so much more. We have seen lives transformed and many people have written their stories giving us their permission to share them with others. As we reflect on this first eight months we realise that the surface can barely be touched in one small book. However, we feel that what God has done is too marvellous and too precious not to be shared so that many can glorify him, and rejoice with us, that we are privileged to be in this generation.

We have always been grateful to God for those accounts of renewal in history where trouble was taken to find out, record, reflect on and write about significant times of God's blessing. If we are not the generation to see Christ return then we hope our small effort will help future generations to reflect on God's ways with them.

It 'seems good to us, and the Holy Spirit', then, that we record for others the amazing story of God's blessing in the North-East of England, centred upon the Sunderland Christian Centre. We are aware that many of the stories we share can be replicated in other parts of the country. There has been such a widespread move of the Spirit. However, there seems to us a number of unique features of the outpouring on Sunderland.

• Sunderland has been a place used by God in other periods of spiritual outpouring. We explore this in the chapter 'Redigging the Well'.

• The prolonged nature of the renewal has been nothing short of astonishing. Nightly meetings with between 200–700 people have continued with no sign of a waning in the intensity of the felt presence of God.

• The cross-denominational nature of this move of God has been a delight. Christians from many churches of all denominations have been joined together.

• Although centred on Sunderland, the renewal has not been located in just one city, but has become a regional work of God.

On methods and such-like

We do need to say something regarding methodology. We are not pretending that this brief telling of the Sunderland story is either comprehensive or 'scientific' in its 'sample'. Literally thousands have passed through the renewal meetings and in many and varied ways God has touched people. Some have only attended once and have been profoundly met. Others have 'soaked' night after night with a long process of inner dealings with God. Our sources of information are quite simply those people who have talked to us, whom we have interviewed, who have written down their experiences or who have given us some insight into their hearts. Some people have kept a fairly meticulous journal as a part of their spiritual walk. We are grateful for those who have allowed us the privileged sight of some of those journal entries.

We are aware that many of the stories will never be told. We are sure that numerous of them will have had the most profound life-changing consequences. It is simply that we did not have access to them. Undoubtedly, in heaven there will be much story-telling.

It is also worth noting that people tell their story in one of two basic ways. In some cases the story is told as a fairly instantaneous reaction to some spiritual revelation or gift: in other words, stories told in the immediacy and freshness of new experience. In these cases little time has passed for any thoughtful reflection. The validity of the story is the immediacy of what a person was experiencing, feeling and seeing. A rich spiritual experience can have a 'dream-like' quality to it even weeks later. Did it really happen? Was I imagining it? To 'catch' the experience whilst it is fresh, whilst lacking mature reflection, is of great benefit.

Other stories are told as a reflection some months down the road. In these instances people, having had an experience, have thought through, prayed through, talked through and tested that which happened to them. People in this way develop a 'paradigm', a working model through which to interpret experience. This type of story-telling has the virtue of considered reflection and provides a good basis for testing the fruit of experience. Both types give the Sunderland story something of richness.

In the nature of things many of the experiences people have entered during the refreshing have been deeply personal. It has been one of the aims of the leaders at SCC to make the renewal meetings a 'place of safety', where people can interact with God, allowing him to do deep, and sometimes painful, things. Some issues have been so deep that it has been inappropriate to testify publicly because of the extremely sensitive nature of the situation. In consequence, we have written things which have never been heard before but to which some dear person wishes to give testimony.

In the main we have used the first names of people who have shared with us. In some cases we have changed names to provide an element of anonymity, indicating where we have done so in the text by the use of an asterisk (eg John* said . . .). However, none of the stories are fictional. These are the true life stories of those whom God has refreshed in the Spirit.

CHAPTER 1

MY SOUL THIRSTS FOR YOU

... no sooner had he [George Whitefield] begun (in the application of his sermon) to invite sinners to believe in Christ, than four persons sank down close to him, almost in the same moment. One of them lay without either sense or motion. A second trembled exceedingly. The third had strong convulsions all over his body, but made no noise, unless by groans. The fourth, equally convulsed, called upon God, with strong cries and tears. From this time, I trust, we shall all suffer God to carry on his own work in the way that pleases him.[1]

'Get to Sunderland, follow the signs for the Port. It's past a few roundabouts. Then it's this big building . . . You can't miss it. I think it's called "New Life Centre".'

That was about all the instruction our dear friend Dorothy gave to us. Consequently it took us some time to actually find Sunderland Christian Centre. Our only previous visits to Sunderland were a trip to the 'Sunderland Illuminations' (a rather good imitation of Blackpool's!) some years before and a few preaching appointments on the other side of the River Wear.

---

[1] John Wesley journal entry for July 7th 1995. *John Wesley's Journal* abridged by Percy Livingstone Parker, 1902, 1993 edition Hodder and Stoughton, London.

Dorothy, who shares with her husband Randy, a local Anglican priest, in the *Northumbria Centre of Prayer for Christian Healing* was one of three reliable and trusted Christians who all said the same thing to us within the space of a week in August 1994 . . . 'God is visiting Sunderland. You must go'.

On the 2nd September we made our first visit to SCC. Sunderland is about thirty-five miles from where we live in the Tyne Valley. Looking back, we are not too sure what we expected. We had been told to arrive early for parking and a seat, but were amazed to find half an hour before the meeting a compound full of cars four abreast. It was also something of a shock to see the eight foot fence around the car park patrolled by security guards, one of whom had an Alsatian dog! Our second shock was to find, on entering the building, about six hundred people worshipping God with amazing enthusiasm. Surely six hundred people didn't want to be in church on a Friday night!

Needless to say, parking was not easy! Nor was finding a seat, as we found ourselves near the back of the five to six hundred strong crowd. But there was something more than the sheer difference of Christians arriving early for a meeting. The 'buzz' in the air, a sense of anticipation which you could almost touch, and people radiant and excited about God made a deep impression on us. Whatever was going on had the quality of electrifying newness about it.

Now, in early May 1995, as we look back at the last eight months in awe, we can only echo the words of Mary: 'My soul magnifies the Lord, and my spirit rejoices in God my Saviour' (Luke 1: 47). God has done so much!

We had experienced renewal ten years previously when the teachings of John Wimber had swept the UK. At that time we had seen many marvellous things happen in the

Baptist church in which we were ministering. However, the last few years had been spiritually dry ones, an experience which we later found out was common to many. Andy was no longer going to be a stipendiary minister but was going to 'tent-make', working on research in social ethics at Glasgow University. Alongside this we were amongst a number of families exploring a new home-based church in Hexham, a picturesque market town in Northumberland, where a number of our close friends lived.

Our stories inevitably overlap, and yet at the same time are deeply personal. We want to tell them individually.

Andy's story

'Brother Andrew, would you speak to our Sunday school this morning. I know you've not prepared, but just share with us what's happening in England,' Mike said as I met him in the car park.

Mike Corriero is pastor to a growing independent charismatic fellowship on the outskirts of the city of Ithaca, NY. For British people it's sometimes hard to grasp the sheer size of the United States. The city of Ithaca is a six hour drive from New York City and still within the same state. In fact, you can drive another three or four hours beyond Ithaca, still in New York State, before you hit either Lake Ontario to the north, or Lake Erie to the south. Mike's strong Brooklyn accent in 'centrally isolated' Ithaca is as jarring to locals as a Geordie in Kent! When we first met, between his Brooklyn and my British accent conversations were pretty stilted. 'Say what, Andy?', and 'I'm sorry Mike I didn't quite catch that . . .' punctuated our attempts at communication.

Nevertheless, from the first time we met there was the instantaneous and beautiful bond of Christian brothers.

Our conversation in the car park came after Jane and I had been in the refreshing for just two short weeks. Already at home we had experienced amazing things. In the few days I had been in Ithaca we had already seen powerful demonstrations of the Spirit. We were excited, 'keyed-up' and ready for God's blessing.

That morning at Agape Bible Church, in the pre-service adult Sunday school there was a sense of expectation that you could almost physically touch. By the time of the service I was finding it difficult to stand upright as wave upon wave of the Holy Spirit washed over me. A young man just behind me began to laugh. I turned to him and simply asked his name. 'Brian, the Holy Spirit is resting on you: would you like some more?' The young man collapsed and spent most of the meeting on the floor. Even before the sermon people were coming forward for prayer in response to a 'word of knowledge'. After the message as people responded to God's loving presence, somewhere in the region of 80% of the 140 congregation had drunk deeply of the Spirit of God. In this small congregation, tucked away in New York State, we observed and experienced the same phenomena which had swept Toronto in January, London in May, Sunderland in August, and many other places at different times since.

Looking back, it seems as if we have been in the river of God forever! Since September 2nd 1994, at least three times a week Jane and I have gathered with God's hungry and thirsty people to seek more of his blessing.

Yet in truth, before that time I was in a fairly flat state spiritually speaking. I had been pastor of two small churches for three and ten years respectively and had just come to the end of a reasonably successful ministry. We had known renewal, seen healings of many kinds, and had seen a number of people come to Christ (between 50–60 in ten years). But by the summer of 1994 I was just about 'burnt-out'. Sometime in early summer I can remember saying to Jane that I felt as if there was nothing left I could give. I was glad to have been a pastor, I would not have missed leading any one of those people to Christ, nor would I have traded the experience of baptism in the Spirit at theological college, nor the renewed outpouring during the John Wimber meetings of the mid '80s. But in the summer of 1994 there was no 'oil left in the jar'.

In August, just before we went to the Highlands of Scotland for our family vacation, our good friend Stuart called to say that 'Something is happening in Sunderland. God is doing great things! Shall we go and see?' To be honest, it was the last thing I wanted to hear. A quiet life in which I knew God's tender care, good health and enough to get by on were on my agenda at that point. I enjoyed the hills and lochs of Scotland without giving Sunderland much thought.

When we returned, the buzz about Sunderland had not gone away. Three other significant people to us called us to 'insist' that we go to Sunderland. Our two boys were planning to go to the youth camp 'Harvest' near Bishop Auckland in County Durham. We dropped them on the Wednesday, helped them put up their tent and left them to what was to become a life-changing few days for both of them.

On the Friday we decided to go to Sunderland, giving in to pressure from our friends, probably as much as anything to be able to say 'We've been, now leave us alone!' We were not prepared for what met us.

Worship was accompanied by strange happenings. A girl on the platform, one of the singers, kept making movements that resembled a chicken—her head kept bobbing up and down in the strangest fashion. It caught my attention. Various people around the room were shaking. Some began to laugh. I had been in charismatic circles for some time and renewal phenomena were not new to me. Much of it I had seen before. And yet there was something of a difference in what I was observing. Ken Gott stood to preach and fell down. Two men hastily jumped up to help Ken regain his feet. The three fell down. This happened for some time until Ken seemed to gain a a little equilibrium. His text was the woman with the issue of blood (Luke 8:43ff).

Outwardly I tried to appear calm: after all I was a charismatic pastor. Inwardly, I was trembling. As Ken read that the woman came trembling to Jesus, and poured out her heart to him, a realisation dawned upon me that I was in the story. It felt as if there was only myself and God in the room. The words resounded in my mind. I was dry, burnt out, a little cynical, desperately in need of God and inwardly trembling.

During the ministry time which followed the preaching Ken asked any pastors to come forward. I literally ran forward, trying not to step on the many bodies which lay in my path. I waited patiently in line. Ken touched me and said 'Lord, give him more'. Instantly my arms tingled all over. Ken's second prayer 'Double it, Lord' sent me to the ground. I had never felt such an influx of divine power and grace. It was, at once, both violent and completely peaceful.

Lying on the floor with a most beautiful sense of the presence of God I realised that my right arm was twitching. I felt somehow detached from it, and was faintly amused. Then I realised that each time I heard Ken say 'more Lord', with those with whom he was praying, my armed twitched more pronouncedly. Then both arms began to twitch, then both legs began to leave the floor. It was a strange sensation, not at all painful, just different and utterly tranquil.

After some time I tried to get up without much success,

my legs having turned completely to jelly. When I eventually could stand, it was only to find out that I could not reply to a question asked by a friend who had spotted me. I heard his request, processed an answer but nothing would come out of my mouth. In the end my friend gave up. 'Andy, I'll call you!' I spent the next forty-eight hours in a more or less pleasantly drunken state. Later it interested me to read an account of the 1907 revival in Sunderland. Donald Gee made this comment:

> Sometimes those newly-filled with the Spirit would go home in the small hours of the morning as outwardly intoxicated as those who had been drinking the wine of this world.[2]

We had entered a similar time of God's blessing. It was the beginning of the most spiritually intense period of my Christian life.

When we picked up our boys from their camp it was to discover that on the very night in which we entered the renewal, around 500 young people had been overwhelmed by the Spirit and found themselves falling to the floor in the large tent used for celebrations, including James and Ben. It was for them, too, the beginning of a great adventure with God.

Our daughter Rebekah was herself deeply affected during my subsequent trip to the USA. I called home each night to find out what was happening to the family. In my absence the family 'abandoned ship' and travelled to Sunderland many nights eager for God's blessing. The touch of God on Rebekah was so profound we tell her story in a later chapter.

---

[2] Donald Gee, *Wind and Flame*, (Heath Press Ltd: Croydon, 1967), first published as *The Pentecostal Movement*, 1941, p 23.

I decided to keep a daily journal of what was happening. From my reading of church history I knew that any move of God is time-limited. Some revivals lasted only a few months, others a year or so. I had an instinctive feeling that this was something important and not to be missed and so it seemed right to record what was happening. I recorded the physical things which happened to me, their kind and intensity, the inward feelings associated with those times of being with God, and any words which were given, both from the Scriptures and prophetically.

Reading those journal entries now tells me that God was giving new revelation and blessing on a daily basis. It had been a very intense time. I recorded various limbs twitching and convulsing, intense and stomach-wrenching laughter. My journal speaks of 'each day a new vitality in reading Scripture'.

On September 14th I recorded a word from God which came very clearly during worship: 'The time of observation is over. Now is the time for participation.' It marked a new beginning, part of which was to ask Ken Gott to pray with us as a couple together. For me (Jane tells her own story) it was a profound experience. Ken placed his hand on my chest and prayed simply 'God, the same that is on me, put on him.'

The effect was instantaneous. I do not remember falling to the floor. I do, however, remember the most incredible pressure on my chest. We have watched and enjoyed the TV programme *Casualty* many times. *Casualty* chronicles the day-to-day life of a busy hospital Accident and Emergency Department. Almost every week some poor patient has to be resuscitated by the use of an electronic device, a 'defibrillator', which sends a bolt of electricity through the body. When applied the body jumps from the table. What happened to me that night *felt* like a scene from *Casualty*. Each time Ken prayed my body literally left the floor. I had never known such spiritual power and infilling.

Other journal entries contain things too personal and too deep for inclusion here, some of which have yet to be worked out. Simply put, God has never been more real, more present and more available.

Though I had been baptised in the Spirit on more than one occasion and had seen people fall in response to prayer, it had never happened to me, personally, until September 2nd 1994. It had always puzzled me. Like many my thoughts on it were, 'It's OK if it happens and if it's of God. But there should be no expectation of it and we ought to be careful about pushing people over.' I had seen on TV whilst in the States what looked like straight-forward manipulation and a good shove!

Over the months of our involvement in the Sunderland renewal I cannot report that I have never had a 'down day'. There have been some very real challenges both in outward circumstances and in inward temptations and dealings with God. What I am sure of, however, is the way God has dealt with me at a deep level, the level of soul and spirit. Part of the fruit for Jane and myself has been the writing of *The Kiss of Intimacy*, which contains our reflections on the deepening of relationship with Jesus through the Song of Songs.[3] Even if the renewal had affected no other person, my personal testimony would be that God has drawn me closer to himself and given a greater passion for his Son. For that it has all been worth it. I am more than ever convinced of his utter goodness and total love.

---

[3] Andy and Jane Fitz-Gibbon, *The Kiss of Intimacy – the Soul's Longing After God: Reflections on the Song of Songs*, (Monarch Publications: Crowborough, 1995)

For me personally, then, the renewal has been a process of receiving a powerful experience of God, observing it in many others, and reflecting biblically, theologically and historically upon it. My conclusion is that we are in the midst of the most far-reaching outpouring of God's Spirit in the UK since 1907–08. If the fruit of the renewal is anything like that following the beginnings of pentecostalism, then the future is indeed bright.

Jane's story

My first reaction on hearing about the renewal at SCC was that I had already been along that path. I was quite content to drift along in the way I was going. Over the last couple of years, I had lost some of the vibrancy I had previously known. Deep inside I knew that I was in need of some spiritual refreshing. So I accompanied Andy and our young daughter, Rebekah, to Sunderland on that Friday in early September 1994.

My feelings were much the same as Andy's. I watched in amazement as although I, too, had seen on many occasions the power of God's Spirit, this was something different. Here was an intensity I had not seen before—it looked as though everyone in the room was being touched. I never doubted that God was working here and most powerfully so, as all over the room people were shaking, jerking, laughing, crying and falling down. Most of the people present ended up lying on the carpet! However, I wasn't sure this was what I wanted, as even on that first visit I knew what I was seeing would demand a high level of commitment. I was content to observe for the time being.

The following evening we went, as promised, to visit our boys at the 'Harvest' teenage camp at Witton Castle. They told us how they had experienced the same things the previous night, as the Spirit had fallen in power on all who were present. That Saturday night the same thing happened. It was an incredible thing to see four hundred teenagers being met by God, and in exactly the same way we had seen the previous night at Sunderland. The same manifestations were present in these young people. As we left the marquee we saw young teenagers sitting on the floor outside the main tent in tears, praying and seeking God. There was a sense of holiness and awe about the whole thing.

Over the next fortnight we went five more times to SCC. I continued to be an onlooker, still not sure that I wanted to participate. However, I felt as if God was saying to me 'Just watch and see how powerful I am.'

The weekend of 16th–18th September found us in the Lake District at a Christian centre for the inaugural weekend of the new fellowship we are part of in Hexham. The same Spirit, with the same power, was present in all the meetings. It was an amazing beginning for the new fellowship (we tell the story more fully later). I decided that whatever God was doing I wanted to be a part of it.

That Sunday evening we found ourselves again in Sunderland. We wanted to be ministered to, especially Andy, as he was leaving for a two week ministry trip to the States early the next morning. Ken Gott prayed with us. I fell down for the first time and Ken prayed some words over me. Later I was amazed to find that they were the same words that were prophetically given to Andy at his ordination some ten years earlier.

Since then we have continued to go several times a week, being committed to the ministry team on Tuesdays, Fridays and Sundays. I never cease to be surprised at how different the meetings are. No two have been alike. Sometimes they are 'wild' with lots of laughter and manifold effects as the Spirit touches people: sometimes almost silent with a real sense of holiness: sometimes lots of prophecy is released and other times none. However, whatever form the meeting has taken, God has always been present and has met people powerfully.

For me a couple of meetings remain in my memory as extra-special. One was early in the renewal when Mary Harrison (see Afterword) prayed with me. It was the first time I showed any manifestations and almost in alarm I asked God what he was doing to me. The second time was when I was prayed with and the Spirit 'hit' me like a bolt of lightning and I was literally knocked off my feet, and again God spoke to me powerfully.

In telling our stories there is much we have *not* included, simply because of space. It has almost, in some ways, been 'too much' and each time we are touched by God we feel 'surely there can't be more'. And yet we are constantly surprised. Eugene Peterson paraphrases Romans 5 in a way which says much for us: 'In alert expectancy such as this, we're never left feeling shortchanged. Quite the contrary—we can't round up enough containers to hold everything God generously pours into our lives through the Holy Spirit!'[4]

Theological reflections

Many things came together during this time. Andy has always had a love of church history. Some years ago he took a research degree in historical theology, his 'specialisation' being the Radical Reformation of the sixteenth century, though he has read more widely. He has often pored over the writings of Jonathan Edwards and others who have experienced revival. He has preached about it,

---

[4] Eugene Peterson, *The Message*, (NavPress: Colorado Springs, 1994), p 370

even longed for it. The astonishing thing was that the very things he had read about he began to see before his eyes.

The phenomena we began to experience had resonances with those things Andy had often pondered in the past. One afternoon Lois Gott called him to ask if he would give a message on the 'history of revivals'. Taking down his much thumbed through copy of Edwards' works, he was amazed to see that some years before he had underlined in different coloured pencils those things which at the time had deeply touched him. They were the very things we had begun to experience at Sunderland.

In the opening thoughts of his *Some Thoughts Concerning the Present Revival of Religion in New England* Edwards comments, 'I make it my rule to lay hold of light and embrace it, wherever I see it, though held forth by a child or an enemy.'[5]

Since first reading Edwards we have always loved his spirit. As we read Edwards again our hearts warmed to much that he said. He spoke about testing any work according to the word of God: of God intermingling in his providence stumbling-blocks with the work, and that human frailty always occurs in a genuine move of God. In other words, in an outpouring of the Spirit, if the general trend of the movement accords with the Scriptures then we should not expect perfection in it. It was an early criticism of the work at Sunderland by some that they were sure they had observed 'the flesh ' in the meeting they had attended.

The idea of 'the flesh' is prominent in Paul's writing in the New Testament. However, it is a fairly tricky term to understand as Paul uses it in a number of different ways. Sometimes, it simply refers to the human body. Other

---

[5] Jonathan Edwards, *Some Thoughts Concerning the Present Revival of Religion in New England*, The Works of Jonathan Edwards, Vol. 1, ed. Edward Hikman, (Banner of Truth Edition: Edinburgh, 1974), p 365.

times it seems to refer to the darker side of human personality. The NIV attempts to shed light by sometimes translating 'flesh' as the 'natural' and other times as the 'sinful nature'. In those senses, particularly the latter, Christians have sought to avoid anything to do with the 'sinful nature'. Some have suggested that the manifestations in the renewal meetings, rather than being of the Holy Spirit, have been a demonstration of something merely natural, or worse, something sinful.

If we read Edwards correctly, he would have been more surprised *not* to have seen human nature, even sinful human nature in the meeting! Lois Gott urged newcomers more than once, 'Be careful in judging what you see. Your censorious, judgemental flesh may be no more sanctified than that other person's attention-seeking flesh'.

It was also something of Edwards' contention that God used what we have termed the 'nameless and faceless'. In his observation, God had greatly used young and inexperienced ministers in the revival. Similarly, in the renewal at Sunderland God has profoundly changed and greatly used many ordinary people. One of the leaders commented over lunch one day that if the ministry team sometimes knew who it was they were praying for they might never have started! Ordinary church folk, many of them young people, have been seen happily praying over denominational leaders both from the UK and abroad. The renewal has produced a levelling amongst God's people. It has been commented upon many times that the way into the refreshing is always through humility. Those who come to observe as either being 'together' or 'knowing all' are often left on the banks whilst thirsty and humbled saints are swimming in the depths.

Since the beginning of the present renewal there has been a sense that it is 'nameless and faceless'. There have not been any particular names associated with the refreshing. It has been a groundswell of the Spirit touching all levels of church life and across all denominations. There are no great theologians or charismatic personalities who have sprung to prominence. In this regard the renewal is much like the beginnings of Pentecostalism. Donald Gee noted that, unlike some other movements in the history of the church, Pentecostalism did not owe its origin to any outstanding personality or religious leader.[6] The movement sprang up in many parts of the world simultaneously. In many respects that is how the present renewal at Sunderland has operated. There have, of course, been connections, visits, sharing of stories and the like, but we are convinced it has been a sovereign move of God's Spirit in his own way.

But why do people fall? Someone made the telling comment that it's because they can't stand up! Actually, that is quite near to the truth and has within it a profound theology. Edwards expressed it more eloquently: ' . . . if beholding the image of this glory did so overpower human nature, is it unreasonable to suppose that such a sight of the spiritual glory itself, should have such a powerful effect?'[7]

It reminds us of John's experience on Patmos in the opening chapter of the book of Revelation. Seeing the risen Christ he fell at his feet as if dead.

Furthermore, we are often in danger of putting a limit upon God. We have not, as a general rule, seen the manifestations we are presently seeing as a normal part of our worship services. The danger is that because we have not seen such demonstrations before we conclude that God does not do this kind of thing. We reject the different and the unusual on the simple grounds that we have not seen it before. Edwards again:

---

[6] Donald Gee, *op cit*, p 3.
[7] *Ibid*, p 368.

It is a great fault in us to limit the sovereign all-wise God, whose judgments are a great deep, and his ways past finding out, where he has not limited himself, and in things concerning which he has not told us what his way shall be.[8]

Reading further, we were simply amazed at the contemporary relevance of the observations and comments Edwards made. He describes in great detail what appeared to be happening (people becoming pale, the loss of the use of reason, the loss of appetite, a trance-like state, crying out, falling etc.[9]) and the effects people felt within themselves, which were universally of love for Christ and the sight and sense of the divine glory. It was as if Edwards was describing the nightly meetings at Sunderland. Space forbids any further comment, suffice it to say that re-reading the history of revivals only served to confirm our belief that we were experiencing a true work of the Spirit of God. Others had passed this way before and, in God's goodness to us, they recorded their experience and mature reflections. Thank God!

On occasion there has been criticism that there is too much emotion associated with the refreshing. On a local '10.30-at-night' TV documentary covering the renewal (remarkably well) the reporter interviewed a 'theologian' whose comment was that Christianity has always been a rational religion. In the renewal meetings things were happening which are not always rational. Therefore, in his opinion, the renewal was not a genuine expression of Christianity. Undoubtedly, there is that which is rational about the Christian faith. But many of its central tenets have an element of 'trans-rationality' about them. Historical events such as the virgin birth and the resurrection, and doctrines such as the Trinity are clearly not rational in the

---

[8] *Ibid*, p 369.
[9] See *ibid*, pp 370–371 for a number of detailed accounts.

sense that we can present either a rational justification for them or fully understand them with our finite human minds. Edwards commented that it is:

> false divinity to suppose that religious affections do not appertain to the substance and essence of Christianity. On the contrary, it seems to me that the very life and soul of all true religion consists in them . . . true virtue or holiness has its seat chiefly in the heart rather than in the head.[10]

It was very clear to us from the first meeting we attended that this move of God was dealing with the hearts of people.

Jonathan Edwards seems to exude wisdom. Many of the bodily effects we have seen were experienced in the revival in New England. Seeing people fall down, their bodies convulse or shake violently can be very disturbing to watch. We have heard, more than once, from inquirers 'Surely, God wouldn't do that to people. Is it in the Bible?' Again Edwards faced such questions. One of his many answers was that the Scriptures mostly deal with the state of a person's heart and mind, rather than with the physical state of their bodies.[11] Edwards directed people from the visible and outward to the invisible and inward. In other words there is a necessity to test the fruit which the movement is producing in people's lives.

It impressed us that this was exactly the stance which Ken and Lois Gott had taken at Sunderland. Each night it was carefully explained that the emphasis was not on the physical manifestations occurring but on the work of God on the inside. To confirm this approach each night a number of people are asked to share what God has been doing in their hearts. 'We can see that you are shaking. . .

---

[10] *Ibid*, p 367.
[11] *Ibid*, p 368.

Can you tell us what is going on inside?' From our observation the fruit is almost universally good. Many of the stories in this book were first told as a testimony during the renewal meetings. We have tested the fruit: it tastes of God. Read for yourself!

CHAPTER 2

REDIGGING THE WELL

'The eyes of the religious millions of Great Britain are now fixed upon Sunderland.'

T.B. Barratt, in his journal September 13th 1907.[1]

On 23rd of March 1992 'by gracious command of Her Majesty the Queen on the fortieth anniversary of her accession to the throne' Sunderland became Britain's newest city.

Once famous for its shipbuilding, coal mining, pottery and glassmaking, the character of Sunderland has changed in recent years as it has diversified into new industries and towards tourism.

The industrial heritage of Sunderland dates back to the beginnings of Christianity in the region when glass-makers from Gaul produced the stained glass for the church of St. Peter's. In time, with the growth and stim-ulus of the coal industry, Sunderland became the world's chief shipbuilding town. In 1988 the final shipyard closed with the end of a glorious heritage which stretched back around six hundred years.

Industry is still present in the form of the giant Nissan factory in the new town of Washington, which forms part

[1] In Donald Gee, *Wind and Flame*, (Heath Press Ltd: Croydon, 1967), first published as *The Pentecostal Movement*, 1941, p 22.

of the city. However, along the banks of the Wear, where once the heavy engineering plant of shipbuilding stretched for several miles, there is now much greenery as the riverside returns to nature (replete with tracks for the discerning tourist!).

Early in the renewal there came a deep feeling of the significance of a move of God in Sunderland. Not the significance of Sunderland Christian Centre, as such, but the city of Sunderland as a place in its own right. There was a sense, which grew quickly to a conviction, that God was visiting a place where he had visited before.

One of the preachers in the early renewal meetings used Genesis 26:18 as his text:

> Isaac dug again the wells of water that had been dug in the days of his father Abraham: for the Philistines had stopped them up after the death of Abraham: and he gave them the names that his father had given them.

There is in the passage a sense of revisiting a place of former blessing and refreshment. And here we were, in the very birthplace of the Pentecostal movement in the UK, drinking deeply again at a well of the Holy Spirit. The realisation dawned . . . a well was being dug that our forebears had dug before.

Celtic beginnings

The Celtic church in England was, we believe, a dynamic move of the Holy Spirit. Much that later characterised the church in the Middle Ages, and for which it has been duly criticised, was absent from its Celtic expression. The Celts were characterised by a zeal for evangelism, an emphasis on brotherhood, and a deeply held belief in the charismatic dealings of God with his people. They believed profoundly that there was no division between the sacred and the secular. The presence of God was seen to permeate all that they were and did. Many considered them to be vagabonds, the *peregrinati* . . . those called by God in a 'non-structural' way, wandering for the love of Christ at the Spirit's initiative.[2]

Of course, there is always a danger in romanticising the past. We have very little hard, historical fact about the church in those early centuries. The histories we have, chiefly Bede, are quite clearly partisan and written from a position of faith. The historical gap is a difficult one to bridge. Nevertheless, from the little we have we can piece together fragments of an age of spiritual awakening when God's people drank deeply of his Spirit.

Sunderland was an early Celtic centre of the faith. One of the great Celtic saints was Hilda who was called by Aidan in 647 AD to found a Christian community on the north bank of the River Wear. From there she went firstly to Hartlepool and then to Whitby where she hosted, in 664 AD, the great and historical Synod between Roman and Celtic streams of Christianity. Little is known of her, but by all accounts she was a Christian of outstanding character and achieved a stature in the church of her day which no woman in Britain has equalled since. Of her pupils five became future bishops of the church. According to Bede 'so great was her prudence that not only ordinary people but also kings and princes sometimes sought and received her counsel when in difficulties . . . she provided . . . an opportunity for salvation and repentance to many who lived far away and who heard the happy story of her industry and virtue.' The work that Hilda had begun was consolidated in 673 when Benedict Biscop and Coelfrith

---

[2] We are grateful to our good friend Roy Searle, of the Northumbria Community, for this understanding of the Celtic saints.

founded the monastery at St. Peter, Monkwearmouth. A well of God's blessing had been dug.

If you visit Whitby Abbey on the North Yorkshire coast (as we had opportunity to do in February 1995), there is a wonderful description of the vibrancy of the Celtic missionaries. Poring over the wall charts caused our pulses to race as we read of Sunderland and a move of God centuries before this one. God in his sovereign grace had dug a well. It sounds strange to tell, but we sensed a deep spiritual connection with those communities of God's Spirit-filled people so long ago.

Turn of the century stirrings

Needless to say, there has been the presence of God's people in Sunderland in every generation, with much faithful work done in Christ's name. However, the well was significantly dug again in 1907. The turn of the twentieth century saw the Christian church at something of a crossroads. Learning was advancing at an amazing pace. New theories in science, politics, psychology and the nature of the Bible were everywhere causing major breakthroughs in all aspects of knowledge. The church was struggling with the many paradigm shifts that were shaking society.

Mainline churches all but gave in to the spirit of the age. Some abandoned the gospel as outmoded. In the West all the major historical denominations, both dissenting and established, trace the beginnings of decline to the first decades of the new century. They have not yet recovered from that decline.

But God had a new agenda, unrecognised at the time but which has had far-reaching and profound effects on the whole world. It is a matter of historical fact that Pentecostalism began when the established churches began to decline.

The mid-to-late nineteenth century saw ferment in the Christian church with regard to the call to holiness. The mid-decades saw revivals in Ulster and parts of the USA. Much was accomplished through the travelling ministries of Charles Finney, D.L. Moody and others. There were greatly blessed pulpit ministries with the likes of C.H. Spurgeon whilst the Keswick movement gave a great impetus towards a deeper life with God. All these great works of God paved the way for that which was to come later.

Interestingly, when Moody visited Sunderland in 1873, Robert Boyd, of Chicago, wrote of his visit: 'When I got to the rooms of the Y.M.C.A. I found the meeting on fire. The young men were speaking in tongues and prophesying.'[3]

As far as we know speaking in tongues was not a common feature of Moody's meetings and this instance, perhaps, prefigured that which was to take place three decades later.

There was excitement in many parts of the church. The most extraordinary manifestations were often observed in the meetings of the Salvation Army. In Newcastle-upon-Tyne, the nearest city to Sunderland, the special correspondent of the *Newcastle Daily Chronicle* in May 1879 covered the story of an all-night meeting. The correspondent was not too sympathetic with the 'goings-on', but his account is quite helpful for us to catch a glimpse of earlier renewal meetings. He begins: 'It is a lamentable confession to make, but my present business is to describe the indescribable . . . [a task that we have faced in writing the Sunderland Story!].

After describing the hall, the participants and much

---

[3] In Michael Harper, *The Twentieth Century Pentecostal Revival*, (Hodder and Stoughton: London, 1965), pp 25–26.

singing, which increased in exuberance, the correspondent continues:

> This chorus might have been sung perhaps a dozen times when there was a shrill scream, a bustle around the platform, and a general rise of the audience. Seats were mounted: hands were raised in the air: the singing was mingled with loud 'hallelujahs', bursts of vociferous prayer, shouting and hysterical laughter. To add to the confusion four of the forms fell backwards, and threw their occupants into the common heap on the floor. So great was the commotion in the centre of the room, so terrifying was the din, that this incidence, which would have thrown an ordinary congregation into uproar, passed almost unnoticed. Sinners were creeping to the penitent form: the Salvation Army was rejoicing: fully one third of those present acted as if they were more or less insane ... Several figures are bent double near the platform, groaning and wringing their hands ...

The account is long and involved, sometimes amusing and well worth a full read. However, we will include just one other excerpt.

> [I] struggled through the crowd to get a look at the penitents. They had fainted away. Here lay a woman in a dead swoon, with six 'hallelujah lasses' singing around her, and not one of them trying to bring her round even by so much as sprinkling water on her face. On the other side of the platform was a man lying full length, his limbs twitching, his lips foaming, totally unregarded ... the 'General' [Booth] was leading the singing ... the penitents whose repentance had been the cause of so much rejoicing were lying unconscious ...

Though the 'special correspondent' was clearly unnerved by the meeting, he describes fairly (besides his use of adjectives!) a renewal meeting similar to those we have recently experienced.

At the turn of the century those who discerned the times began to pray for a new spiritual awakening. It came in 1904 in Wales. Revival broke out and it heartened believers the world over. If God could visit Wales, he could visit any place. The heart-cry of many was 'Why Wales only? Why not other lands? Why not world wide revival?'[4]

The birth of Pentecostalism

Preachers from Britain made their way to the USA. By 1905 F.B. Meyer was announcing the good news of revival in Los Angeles and 1906 saw the beginnings of the three year long Azusa Street revival. Pentecostalism was born.

It is, though, oversimplifying things to attribute the whole move of God to Los Angeles. T. B. Barratt, an Englishman who had lived most of his life in Norway and was currently a Methodist preacher, was baptised in the Spirit in the same year, not on the West Coast but rather in New York. Though personally he never visited Azusa Street he entered into correspondence with those in the middle of revival. On October 7th 1906, at 5 pm, T.B. Barratt received the power of God, after having fasted and prayed for the day.

Barratt was by no means the only believer, apart from the Azusa Street awakening, to be baptised in the Spirit during these formative years of the new century. There were various outpourings of the Spirit in 1906 in other places too. Interestingly, in the same year there were similar manifestations of spiritual power in Toronto.[5] We

---

[4] See Donald Gee, *op cit*, p 6.

[5] Donald Gee, *op cit* p13.

mention Barratt, however, because of his close connection with Sunderland and Alexander Boddy, the vicar of All Saints, Monkwearmouth.

Alexander Boddy had been vicar of All Saints since 1886, following a two year curacy. He remained in the parish until 1922, a thirty-eight year ministry in one place—almost inconceivable for us now in a generation defined by mobility.

Boddy was an interesting man who, besides his involvement in the Keswick movement, was an accomplished traveller, writer and Fellow of The Royal Geographical Society (which he later saw as something of a distraction from Christ[6]).

The Welsh revival fascinated Boddy and he was one of many earnest 'seekers' who made the trip to South Wales to see for themselves. In 1906 Boddy began a prayer meeting in the vestry of All Saints. 'We were tarrying until we should be endued with power from on high', he commented.[7] He also heard of the work of T.B. Barratt in Norway and visited Oslo in March 1907. The outpouring of God's Spirit upon that nation affected Boddy even more than his visit to Evan Roberts at Tonypandy.[8] In comparing the two he perceived that there was more spiritual power in the Norway awakening than in the Welsh revival.[9] Boddy wanted Barratt to visit Sunderland and succeeded in arranging a trip for the end of August 1907. Precise chronicling of events is difficult although it seems that either that same night at the prayer meeting or the next evening at an 'after-meeting', the first three members of Boddy's congregation were baptised in the

[6] William K. Kay, *Inside Story*, (Mattersey Hall Publishing: Mattersey, 1990), p 18.
[7] *Ibid*, p 19.
[8] See Donald Gee, *op cit*, p 20.
[9] William Kay, *op cit*, p 21.

Spirit accompanied by the gift of tongues.[10] Meetings were held in the parish hall every afternoon and evening, with each service followed by a 'waiting meeting' for those who desired the fullness of the Spirit.[11]

Barratt stayed with Boddy for seven weeks and meetings were held in the vestry of All Saints Church. By all accounts the meetings were quite orderly (a little 'flat' for visitors from the Salvation Army!). However, many visited Sunderland and were inflamed by the power of God.

The numbers recorded were not great. Even in Oslo, where Boddy first encountered the Pentecostal awakening there were only around 120 at the meeting. Back in Sunderland there were as few as four who gathered to pray before Barratt's visit in 1907. After the first fortnight of Barratt's ministry around fourteen had been baptised in the Spirit accompanied by speaking in tongues.[12] According to Boddy between September 1907 and April 1908 there were around 500 people who had been baptised in the Spirit through some contact with Sunderland.[13]

The Sunderland Echo carried the story of the renewal meetings. In September 1907 there was this report:

The Happiest Day I've Had

Suddenly a dark gentleman who had been sitting quietly at the side of the hall started a revival hymn, which was sung with vigour by the congregation, many of whom were on their knees. The hymn ended, and the dark gentleman began in fervid tones to ask that the spirit of Christ might come into the hall. While so engaged he

---

[10] See Michael Harper, *op cit*, p 38.

[11] Donald Gee, *op cit*, p 22.

[12] *Ibid*, p 22.

[13] *Ibid*, p 29.

burst into loud shouts and instantly the bulk of those present broke into exclamations led by a gentleman with a powerful bass voice who repeatedly exclaimed 'He is here, He is here.' The dark gentleman continued to laugh strongly, and said, 'I can't help doing it I am so happy. It's the happiest day I've had.'

'Hallelujah, hallelujah,' was shouted from all parts of the building. Ladies were burying their faces in their hands as they knelt at the forms, and the excitement was intense.

Over the months that followed there were many visitors to Sunderland. Correspondence was great and Boddy employed two secretaries to answer mail. At Pentecost 1908 Boddy held a Whitsuntide Conference, the first of many, and began to publish *Confidence*, a magazine committed to exploring the new phenomena and teachings of Pentecostalism. The magazine ran from April 1908 until 1926 with 141 issues altogether.

Among the early and significant visitors to Sunderland was Smith Wigglesworth. Though at first unimpressed by Boddy's meetings (Wigglesworth had been used to the more effervescent Salvation Army style), after being prayed with by Mary Boddy he received an experience of the fullness of the Spirit. Subsequently Wigglesworth travelled to many parts of the UK and abroad to the USA, the Belgian Congo, Palestine, Denmark, Sweden, Ceylon, Australia and New Zealand.[14] In his ministry alone can be seen the profound influence that the renewal at Sunderland was to have worldwide. Wigglesworth, though perhaps the most famous, was merely one of many.

---

[14] See *Alexander Boddy, Pastor and Prophet*, (Wearside Historic Churches Group, All Saints' PCC: Monkwearmouth, Sunderland, 1986), pp 63–64.

Wells of God's blessing

It seems that in times of spiritual awakening God particularly blesses certain places which then draw people from many parts. These places become like spiritual wells to God's thirsty people. It had happened in South Wales in 1904, at Azusa Street in 1906, and in Sunderland in 1907. It had happened before, for instance at Llangeitho, under the ministry of Daniel Rowlands, when during a period of forty-nine years there were seven outpourings of the Spirit at regular seven year intervals.[15]

Beyond a shadow of doubt Toronto has become such a well. Many have travelled from all over the world, received refreshing from God and carried the torch back to their home churches. Some who carry the torch are then used by God to dig a well, which in turn becomes a centre for those seeking God's touch.

Equally, we are sure that Sunderland has become such a well. We are uncertain how many people have come through Sunderland over the months, but a conservative estimate of the number of people attending the renewal meetings in the first eight months is in the region of 50,000. One of the amazing things for us is to see the number of folk seeking God night after night. They have come from all parts of the United Kingdom, from Holland, Austria, Australia, Bosnia, the USA, New Zealand, Norway, Switzerland, Malaysia, Canada, France and other places.

We have pondered the question 'Why Sunderland?' What is it about this place in the North-East of England which causes God to visit it again and again? We can never be certain in our answer, always willing to give way to the sovereignty of God. God's ways are truly past finding out, his thoughts are not our thoughts.

---

[15] See John Owen, *A Memoir of Daniel Rowlands of Llangeitho*, (Banner of Truth Trust, 1981), reprinted from 1848, p 48.

And yet Michael Harper had a valuable insight in his useful little book *The Twentieth Century Pentecostal Revival*[16]: 'The Pentecostal Movement was born in a stable. So was Christianity.'[17]

Sunderland has in many ways been that stable. The Christian church has a way of looking back with fondest memories on those who, in their time, were deeply radical yet who at the time were subject to misunderstanding, criticism and sometimes ridicule. It was prophesied over Ken Gott in Toronto, by Marc Du Pont, that God was giving to Ken the ministry of the baby Jesus. It puzzled Ken. By natural temperament he would have preferred the ministry of the 'healing' Jesus, or the Jesus of signs and wonders, or even the great teacher. But the baby Jesus . . . what could that mean? It has become clear to many of us associated with the renewal at Sunderland. 'Shepherds and wise men', adults and children, religious leaders and unbelievers have travelled in their thousands to see that which God has been doing at the stable, not now in Bethlehem, but the equally unlikely surroundings of Hendon in Sunderland.

The rest of this book is testimony to God's goodness in people's lives in times of refreshing.

---

[16] Michael Harper, *The Twentieth Century Pentecostal Revival*, (Hodder and Stoughton: London, 1965).
[17] *Ibid*, p 23.

CHAPTER 3

RENEWED DAY BY DAY

Clearly it is the saints, not the sinners, that are primarily involved in revival. The quickening of the saints is the root, while the saving of the sinners is the fruit.[1]

Perhaps the most common fruit of the renewal has been the number of people who have found a renewed passion for Christ. If it has been said once, it has been said a thousand times that in the renewal God has radicalised the love of his people. Many of the testimonies we have received and heard contain no dramatic incidents and no overwhelming visions of heaven. Yet, in God's goodness, as people have opened their hearts in a new way, God has poured peace, grace and greater love into their hearts. Even for those whose experience has contained more of drama and outward manifestation of the Spirit's presence, love for Christ is the bedrock of that which has been accomplished. A church radically renewed with love for Jesus is a church which has not been seen by the world for a long time.

---

[1] Arthur Wallis, *In the Day of Thy Power*, (Christian Literature Crusade: Alresford, 1956).

Visions of the Saviour

God has moved in people from all walks of life. There is no particular personality type, social class or profession which stand out as having been touched more than others. It is impossible to say 'This is just affecting women' or 'This is only for people without an education'. We have seen God deal with every conceivable type of person.

Early in the renewal John came to a series of meetings addressed by Suzette Hattingh, a personal friend of Lois Gott and a member of Reinhart Bonnke's team. John is an educated man, just turned forty, who is very much at the peak of his profession. He works for a government agency involved in inner-city economic regeneration. John has been a Christian for six years.

His experience was so startling that he wrote it down immediately on his return home. He comments that although there were over 400 people in the room and a great deal of noise (it was a particularly 'wild' night as we remember) he was unaware of distractions. As all his attention was focused on God he became aware of only two people in the room—himself and Jesus.

John records that he had a clear visualisation of Jesus for the first time. In his vision Jesus was asking John to join him. John then poured out to the Lord all his concerns, worries, thoughts and anxieties. He told Jesus about his work-related worries, finances, children, church, time etc.

Jesus assured John that he knew and understood all his worries. John continues his story,

'At that point I became conscious of the room, and people around me, I was lying on my back. It took me a while to get my bearings, and I sat up feeling dazed. I was aware of [a member of the ministry team and personal friend] behind me. He said something like "How are you my old friend?" and started massaging my shoulders, and praying for me.

'I felt as though I was going into a deeper sleep, and finally totally relaxed, not aware of anything other than God's knowledge of me and an overwhelming feeling of being loved and cared for.

'I felt as though I was asleep for a long time, and in that time I visualised an image which I had experienced in the past: that of a maze with many directions, with one direct path from the edge of the maze to the centre, and there are two seats, where Jesus and I are talking.

'It was as though Jesus was quickly accessible, and whilst he wanted to know of the things in my life, he didn't want them to act as a barrier between myself and him.

'I saw myself waking from this visualisation, although not waking physically. I was aware of Jesus sitting beside me and asking how I felt. Jesus was saying again that he knew how I felt and understood the way I needed to "act out a role" and "put on an act", particularly at work.

'He then gave me a clear message that he wanted other people to see him through me and said "Don't prevent that from happening". All the time Jesus was looking straight into my eyes and said a number of times "Allow me to use you", "Let other people see me through you","Let other people know that I love them". There was so much love and understanding expressed on his face.

'When I finally "came to", I felt overwhelmed by emotion, and a sense of humility and awe that God was wanting to use me to reach other people. And that through his love for me, he was able to free me up from daily pressures, to allow me more scope to be available to God. I also had a feeling of being required to move closer to God, study the word of God and that God would honour that time.'

Correcting vision

God has been clarifying spiritual vision for many as they have received his refreshing. Clive, a quiet and gentle man in his thirties works at the university in horticulture. He tells how God had spoken to him:

'In October God gave me a picture whilst resting in his Spirit. I saw the plates of the earth's crust, shifting and moving to cause an earthquake. God was telling me quietly how he wanted me to align myself, my will, into his way of thinking and doing things. And that if it was to take an earthquake, then that is what he would do in my life.

'So throughout the past months God has been increasingly correcting my vision to see things his way, with his eyes, so that my will is in more perfect alignment with his.

'God has shown me that I have to be utterly dependent on him, to completely trust him, to be wrapped up in him, for Jesus to lavish his love on me, to be enraptured, charmed and filled by his Holy Spirit.'

Clive told us of many other lessons God has taught him—about holiness, of opening 'dark compartments' to God and of being made more pliable and flexible in following Jesus.

A dry and weary land

Many of God's people have been dry. We became aware early in the renewal that it was a common story. Where once the living water of God's Spirit had flowed freely, there was now a virtual drought! Subsequently, for many, to enter the renewal was to find a new place of spiritual refreshment and liberty. The outward manifestation of that has often been laughter.

Elaine expressed her experience as needing to be 'overfilled' with joy before God began a deeper work of release and freeing her from inner dispositions contrary to God. For Elaine one of the areas in which she knew she needed to trust God was in his care for her children. Elaine had laughed many times in God's presence, but one Sunday after praying with someone else she felt as if a 'great huge stopper' had been lifted out of her heart. She said,

'I began to cry and sob in a way that I'd never felt before for [her son], for his life, for his hurt—it felt so deep it actually hurt.'

A prophetic word was spoken over her about releasing her own grip and letting go of her son, for God would never release his grip. Immediately, the stifling burden and heaviness lifted. Her anxiety over her son's future wellbeing was lifted and has been replaced with a more or less continuous peace.

Harvey, similarly, tells of a dry time before the renewal followed by an abundance of life. He had been a Christian since 1987 but was somewhat frustrated. In the summer of 1994 he had begun to be desperate for a new touch of God. When the renewal started Harvey said to God, 'Whatever you want to do, you know my heart.' He continues to describe how he entered the renewal.

'I began to physically react with one knee jerking up. I was a bit scared but knew God was doing something. I said "I don't know what you're doing Lord, but I need a change so I'll go with it." Not long afterwards I collapsed and knocked over a few chairs. I felt like I could burst.

'The next day, and every day since I have desired to pray every morning and read the Bible. I have experienced newness and great life in the secret place of prayer. I see things in the Bible I never saw before. Over the months I believe this has served to be a springboard into much more . . . Life as a Christian has never been more exciting.'

Aldersgate Street again

We have had testimonies from people of all denominations to a wonderful touch from God. Some have told of prophecies of many years ago being fulfilled in the refreshing, of giftings being given and restored.

Bob and Joan are Methodists of some years standing. Bob is a headteacher at a first school and also serves on a local authority committee for religious education. It was during such a meeting that the conversation turned to a new phenomenon sweeping the church. Committee members expressed their views: Bob decided to see for himself. On the way to the meeting he commented to Joan, 'I'm going very reluctantly to Aldersgate Street tonight!' (For those who are not Methodists, it was at Aldersgate Street John Wesley had his profound experience of God when his heart was 'strangely warmed'.) Though hesitant, Bob had an instinctive sense that there was to be a new meeting with God.

Joan and Bob felt at home in the meeting of six hundred or so people singing vigorously 'To God be the glory'. However, when Bob sat down he was not ready for what happened next.

'As I sat down an involuntary guffaw came from my mouth. I looked at Joan in bewilderment as to where it had come from. (I hadn't guffawed much during worship in the last 25 years!) I hardly had time to appreciate or make sense of what was going on, when I suddenly began to laugh, really laugh. It wasn't quiet or secretive, it was "torrential". I am no stranger to laughing but this was new in my experience . . . my laughing lasted at least an hour and a quarter.'

Interestingly, it was on the same night that Lois Gott read from John Wesley's journal illustrating similar happenings during Wesley's preaching.

Bob and Joan made the half hour journey to Sunderland the next night. Being an educator, Bob has been careful to document what happened to him. On his second visit the manifestation of the Spirit was different. As he raised his hands in worship it seemed that something was weighing on them making them very heavy—too heavy to hold up. He remembers commenting to Joan, 'I know I'm getting older—but tired arms—this is ridiculous, I can't hold them up for any length of time'.

Having given up trying to raise his arms Bob found his arms, legs, and whole body beginning to shake in an unstoppable fashion.

On the inside Bob testifies to experiencing God in a wonderful new way. In fact, the inner experience was such that he determined not to mind what was happening externally. Over the months both Joan and Bob feel they have learned to worship God in a new way and have learned what it means to 'abide in him'.

Your young men shall dream dreams

Peter had experienced the Holy Spirit many times. At the renewal in Sunderland his heart was fired again to take the gospel to others. He says, 'My desire is to take the blessing back to my home town and to Africa, especially Kenya.'

Peter's life has not always been smooth. With many in this generation, he had experienced the pain of divorce. In a renewal meeting in the South of England, before he came to Sunderland he encountered God. At that time

God showed him the depths of his grief and made him aware of idolatry and self-deception in his heart. His prayer became, 'Lord, my heart needs a home'.

On his first Sunday morning in the North-East, he felt prompted to go to Sunderland Christian Centre. It turned out to be the first meeting after Ken and Lois Gott had returned from Toronto. Peter found the meeting strange, but was affected by the strong anointing.

'I believe the Lord did a deep work in my spirit both then and at three succeeding meetings at SCC in August.'

In October Peter was able to settle in Sunderland. 'The Lord provided a wonderful place for me to stay with the only Kenyan in the church! He also provided me with a Christian boss and a Christian room-mate at work.'

However, 'Christmas was a very difficult time for me. I was deeply anxious about my future and also longing to have a genuine testimony. On returning to the North-East in the New Year, the Lord revealed to me the key of submission in relationship—I needed to be known and be willing to receive from the Lord through anyone. Since then, I have been developing deeper relationships and have given and received much blessing, answering some of my longings for intimacy and enabling me to trust others and myself more.

'I believe my life will soon have more of an outlet as the Lord has already positioned me regarding social outreach in my home town and ministry in Kenya. I had originally thought that the only thing that I would be taking away from Sunderland would be the work that God had done in my heart, but now I realise there is something more: I will be taking the love of many other people in my heart and I will be leaving my love behind in theirs.'

Steve is another young man from the south of England who found his way to the renewal at Sunderland. Like

Peter, he is involved in work at the university. Steve has three degrees, is presently working on a PhD and is a computer operator by profession. For the four years prior to moving to Sunderland he had lived in Hull. There he had felt God had burdened him for international students—particularly Muslims. He had spent much of those four years involved in evangelism and considered himself 'on fire' for God. However he knew something was missing.

'I knew in my head that God loved me, but not down in my heart. I felt I had to strive to please God to gain acceptance by him. If I did something wrong I had to do some good, practical act to please God, as well as repent. I was also striving to bless other people all the time, as I felt that was the way I gained blessing from God.'

Some friends recommended that Steve try out Sunderland Christian Centre when looking for a local church. He confesses that he had heard a little about the renewal but thought nightly meetings were stupid. . . surely Christians should be out evangelising, not getting blessed! His perceptions changed as he began to attend SCC and started receiving from God.

'God taught me that the most important thing is to flow with what he is doing. It is best to move out in evangelism, receiving or whatever in his timing rather than my own.

'Through "carpet time" the Lord has softened me. I used to have quite a hard heart, and be impatient, liking everything to be done yesterday. This was particularly in praying and ministering to people, when I used to "force" myself upon them. I was one of these zealous, over-enthusiastic Pentecostals. Now, when I pray or chat to people, I feel a gentleness of spirit and compassion towards them. I am gentle rather than going "boom, boom boom".'

Steve liked his respectable professional image. However, God had different ideas. 'The Lord has taken that all away. The last thing I would want to do as a "respectable middle-class English professional" is to be bent double groaning, and lying on the floor kicking my legs up in the air in public, let alone on the TV. I also used to have a problem with submission. The Lord has made me more submissive to him and to leadership. He has also dealt with the striving. I now know that God loves me whatever I do. I don't have to strive to worship or serve him. I am just blown along by the breeze of the Holy Spirit. I let God minister through me, rather than a percentage God and another percentage Steve.

'I no longer shut myself off at work, and all the elements of self-ambition and striving to be a success at work have gone. I have given my PhD over to God. I am not worried about whether or not I get it. I do work, obviously, but no longer as a workaholic. In fact, I find I am doing just as much, if not more, work done in less time in a more peaceful way. I am more effective as I have committed it to the Lord rather than trying myself.'

Steve concludes, 'The Lord has dealt with a striving, self-ambitious workaholic, and turned him into someone who can work effectively for him.'

God changes lives

Phil has been a Christian for six years, but throughout that time he has been battling against feelings of insecurity, rejection and failure. He recognised that God had been changing him over the years but Phil felt that it was very slow. Then, in October 1994, a speaker who was visiting Sunderland from Canada prayed with Phil. He prayed against any feelings of inferiority in Phil's life. It was a turning point which Phil describes:

'I reacted quite strongly to his prayers, and later at home began to feel a surge of power running through my body. Over the weeks I began to experience strong waves of God's power flowing through my life. This brought me real assurance in God and confidence that he is with me and wants to use me to help fulfil his purposes.

'At Sunderland the power of God is being poured out, changing and equipping people for service. As God has quickened his touch on my life, many of the problems that hold me back have come to the surface. God can deal with them and is, in fact, dealing with them right now. God changes lives.'

Be holy

Clearly God is leading people towards holiness in the renewal. Beholding and reflecting the Lord as we rest in his Spirit leads to holy lives. Ken, from Newcastle-upon-Tyne, testifies that God had given him a very clear word about God's desire for clean vessels. He shared the word with his church. The very next night God made the word even more real to Ken.

'The Holy Spirit came upon me and I was flung sideways and lay for at least an hour. No great revelation came before me but the Holy Spirit said, "Now that you are on your face it's time to rid your life of all the dross." I now see the Lord in a different light and he is blessing me beyond measure in this current move of the Spirit.'

Similarly, Derek* told us, 'The first "fruit" I became aware of was a new freedom from the pressure of lustful thoughts. This may seem trivial, but for me this has been important. I had always assumed that the kind of thoughts that flitted in and out of my mind almost continually were just part of the normal "baggage" that men had to contend with. Part of me seemed hostage to these thoughts, sometimes dwelling on them and allowing them to take more shape in my mind than I would ever have wished to admit. Now I am more aware of the holy fear of God than ever before, and I can honestly say that it feels *good*. I really desire God's holiness, and know that I need his grace daily to get there.'

Lifting burdens

Laughter is often a feature of the renewal meetings at Sunderland and is often used by God to lift burdens from those who are carrying them and weighed down.

Max, along with another colleague had been leading their church through an 'interregnum'. They were seeking a new leader and for the time being the burden fell squarely on their shoulders. Pressure began to mount and during one week Max felt a great deal of stress and tension building up inside himself. By the end of the week Max felt worn out and in desperate need of refreshing. He and his friend came to Sunderland.

God's timing is always perfect and Max was asked to share what God had been doing in his life.

'I really didn't get very far before I experienced the "jerks" and the Holy Spirit put me down exceedingly quick!'

That night both Max and his friend helped the ministry team as 'catchers', and as they chatted together towards the end of the meeting, exchanging notes.

'All of a sudden the Holy Spirit hit the pair of us with the joy of laughter. Many people will know me as quite a serious person, but we laughed and laughed and laughed. When we finally calmed down, all the tension, all the stress had been lifted from us both. It made me realise that God can minister to you anytime.'

More on phenomena

Where there has been controversy in renewal movements through the centuries, it usually relates to the physical phenomena often associated with intense spiritual life. It is sometimes wondered, 'Can't we have the fruit of renewal without the visible, often disturbing, manifestations?' For whatever reasons, in the history of revival movements phenomena and fruit have always been experienced together. It makes the movement look somewhat 'untidy' and not always in control. It gives the leaders of the movement frequent cause for reflection on the nature of physical demonstrations and their relationship to the inner work of the Spirit.

One man expressed similar thoughts in this way: 'Even when experiencing the physical phenomena, my only focus is on God and what he is doing in my heart.'

General Bramwell Booth was the son of William Booth, famous founder of the Salvation Army. He wrote an important history of the early days of the 'Army' in which he comments on 'signs and wonders' which occurred in many of their meetings. He reflects that manifestations of the Spirit were fairly common in the work of the Army. He instances the phenomena of falling down as the most common, and, interestingly, that it happened many times to those who were still unsaved. When unbelievers rose after a period of prostration they were invariably converted to Christ, having first been affected by the power of the Spirit.[2] Though people sometimes fell with 'great violence' Booth comments that no one was ever really hurt by the fall. Also, it didn't seem to matter whether folk were old or young, God was no respecter of person.

---

[2] Bramwell Booth, *Echoes and Memories*, (Hodder and Stoughton: London, 1925), pp 52–3.

Booth does comment, however, that when people fell it was the custom at the time to have the person carried out to rest in another room. Also of interest is that Booth made sure there was a doctor on hand to test the genuineness of the prostration, though when this had become a common occurrence the presence of a physician was not thought to be as important.

Like many of us, Booth asked the question as to what the manifestations may mean. He draws a blank but suggests that when God is powerfully present certain people are like 'spiritual conductors' who readily receive the influence from God and correspondingly fall down being unable to stand.[3] Booth also mentions visions being given to those who lay in the presence of God. Strangely and tantalisingly, he mentions 'levitation' in some of the meetings to be well attested. He comments 'Of these, however, I do not write now, except to say that I cannot doubt that everything about them was open and true.'[4] To our knowledge levitation has not yet been seen in the meetings at Sunderland!

Not exactly extrovert

It would be wrong to think that everyone touched by God in the renewal is of outgoing character. Chris teaches at a large Newcastle hospital and in her own words is a 'conservative' who 'doesn't wear her heart on her sleeve' and who is 'not exactly extrovert'. She believed without doubt that the renewal was of God, was herself deeply touched, but admits that she found a little difficulty with some of the outward manifestations. She also finds that the most precious times with God have been on her own in her bedroom where she doesn't feel inhibited.

[3] *Ibid*, p 55.
[4] *Ibid*, p 56.

In one meeting some months into the renewal, however, Chris was met by God in a way unusual for her. During worship she felt as if a heavy weight was pressing her down to her knees. She began to feel very weak and shaky. God spoke clearly, 'Let go!'

She remembers saying to God, 'I'm all right. I don't know what I have to let go of.' God showed her two occasions in her life which had profoundly affected her. In her job she had worked in intensive therapy with a role in which she effectively 'held the reins and thought I was always in control'. The other incident was when her brother was killed by a train. Her parents were so devastated that Chris felt she needed to return home 'to take control'.

Now, in the presence of God, Chris realised that she had to relinquish control to God. She did.

'What happened next was so funny. As I tried to walk away I felt like a spring bouncing up and down. I can't explain how refreshing and releasing it was—yet I was self-conscious. Then one of the men in our church nearby said, "Chris, God has just shown me a picture of a spring which was clogged up and has now been untangled." It was great, I began to laugh at myself more and more.

'The next morning when I woke I just began thanking God for what he'd done. Then I turned to my Bible. I was reading Matthew 20:20 which says, "Then the mother of the sons of Zebedee" and I remembered Zebedee from the "Magic Roundabout"[5] was a spring! Once again I laughed and laughed as well as bobbing up and down. And so God is wonderfully continuing to bless me, and my friends are loving it!'

---

[5] The 'Magic Roundabout' was a children's programme in the 1970s shown just before the six o'clock news. Many adults saw it, and loved it!

The value of keeping a journal

Some people have kept a meticulous journal of all that God has done in them during the renewal, together with their day to day musings on what it all might mean. Simon, Head of Physics in a Tertiary College, husband, father of three, and Baptist deacon and preacher shared some of his journal entries with us. The value of the entries is in the immediacy of the experience and reflection. We include brief 'snippets' from some of his daily thoughts.

> September 1: I need to know more about the 'Toronto Blessing' . . . I have been uneasy about the contagious way it seems to be transmitted. But the signs are impressive, and seem harmless. And the fruit—holiness of life, perception of God's holiness—is good.
>
> September 5: . . . Suppose this is the beginning of the 'big one', it could also have a number of stages, of which this [renewal] would be the first . . . Other aspects could come later . . . The next phase would probably be more prophetic, filling our minds with the truth of God—more my scene! Meanwhile, I should support and be permeated by this Toronto Blessing, which I could certainly do with.
>
> September 21: I went to Sunderland Christian Centre last night, to see the Toronto Blessing at work. It was impressive: I am now convinced that it is of God, and that it is probably the first stage of something bigger, the John the Baptist of a made-to-measure revival, the big one.
>
> September 25: . . . What is happening? The tangible presence of the Lord seems so real, and so close, all the time and in all sorts of places. It can't just be that

we are more responsive to what was there all the time. It must be that in some way God has chosen this time to 'come closer' to us—just as he did in the Incarnation. But why?

October 12: The worship leader [at Sunderland] tonight said that 'the age of superstars is over'. And so it is. God is showering his blessing impartially on large congregations, small fellowships, and in our own upper room, using anyone, not just gifted counsellors, as the 'ministry team'. So there is no need to strive for higher plains of ministry—the Lord isn't working that way anymore . . . A kingdom where every thing and every person is appreciated and valued for what it is, without comparing it to any other thing or person—that's a radical kingdom indeed—but it is part of what God is doing now.

We wish we could include more from Simon's journal, but sadly, space forbids. The complete journal entries display a pilgrimage in renewal which is honest, searching and profoundly insightful.

Difficulties, yet still receiving

Even those who have found it difficult to enter fully into the renewal have discovered God powerfully at work. Eleanor is one such person. She testifies that although she has found it hard (the groaning and shaking simply put her off) she has found God's healing. She was involved in a road accident and suffered severe whiplash and a slipped disc. Whilst signed off work she attended meetings at Sunderland. She writes:

'On Saturday morning [the preacher] asked all those who were in pain to stand up, which I did. He prayed for the pain to go. He then asked for those who had been healed to remain standing. At this time I sat down, because I felt nothing. Then he asked us to stand up again. This time I felt as though there was water running down my back, but I still had the pain. When I came back for the evening session I sang the choruses by looking up at the screen without pain in my back. Praise the Lord!

'On the following Wednesday I went to the doctor, because he had arranged for traction for my back. Instead, he said I could go back to work on the following Monday. I have had no pain since.'

Roy is another person who doesn't experience any manifestations. However, he says, 'I know that the Holy Spirit is being poured out for I love the Lord more than ever before.'

One night was especially significant to Roy. 'I was brought up in a Christian home and gave my heart to the Lord at a young age. But until one night in the renewal meetings I had niggling doubts of who I was in the Lord and whether I was saved. That night I was prayed for and the Holy Spirit showed me a vision of me standing and the Lord putting a crown of gold on my head. I thought he was showing me that I was a prince and a son.'

Some months later whilst Roy was being prayed with he was given a word of prophecy which recalled the vision. God again spoke to him, this time slightly differently, saying that Roy wasn't just a son of the King but to God was as precious as a king. Roy still doesn't show any manifestations, but that is no longer important to him. 'If God wants me to shake then he will do it in his time, to know who I am in Christ and to sit in his presence is precious to me.'

Soaking in God

One of the things we have learnt in the renewal is the value of what has been termed 'soaking in God'. By that we mean a resting in his presence for a prolonged time, continuing to worship and allowing the Spirit to do whatever he wills in our hearts. We have tried to encourage those who have fallen in the Spirit to remain in their prostrated position for as long as they are able. It is often after some time that God does the deepest things.

Peter is a pastor of some experience and first came into contact with the renewal at the Airport Vineyard in the early summer of 1994. Since then, Peter, his wife Ruth and many of their church members have spent many nights in the renewal at Sunderland.

Peter shared some valuable insights on the value of spending quality time in God's presence. Peter jokes that travelling to Sunderland was a hardship, for he has been a lifelong Newcastle United follower![6] He told us:

'We continued to go to Sunderland at least a couple of times each week and found not only that God was there, but the more we seek him the more we find! There is a definite progression in this. The more we pray and are prayed for, the more God comes to us, the more we experience him in our lives and the more of us he has. We really should have known that all along. It took me at any rate more than a few times of ministry to 'break through'. I also discovered that as I went along, each occasion was different to the last, as the Spirit highlighted different areas of need to me. Sometimes there would be quite strong manifestations, at other times hardly any. Sometimes tears, sometimes laughter, sometimes neither. Sometimes peace, melting into the floor, other times a conviction of sinful-

---

[6] The two football teams Newcastle United and Sunderland have a legendary local rivalry.

ness, especially pride in its various forms, and the wonder of God's love and forgiveness, leading to tears of shame followed by tears of joy. Sometimes all I seemed to do was examine the ceiling as I lay on the floor!

'Over the months I have become aware of a greatly increasing sense of God's presence at all times and places, never more so than now. This is especially true during times of worship and on a few remarkable occasions I, or even the whole meeting, have come to an abrupt halt as we are overcome by the presence of the Lord. I have personally discovered a greatly increased enthusiasm and love for God, with decreasing time and inclination for former things—even Newcastle United and the TV! It's as if life has come back into my faith. What I knew in the mind has reached down to my heart. I've come alive again, so to speak, in a way that I wasn't before. I still am not all that I ought to be, but I'm much nearer to it than I ever was.'

Too much to tell

The stories we have briefly told above can be duplicated a hundredfold! Many have told us of radicalised love, of God's little surprises, of overcoming sins and fears, of learning for the first time the love of the Father, of feeling the safety of his loving arms, of people not wanting to go to the meeting but finding the message was just for them. We have heard of visions with life-changing potential— really too much for one small book. As one young woman said, 'In the renewal God even gave me a fabulous boyfriend!' God has simply blessed and refreshed his people.

CHAPTER 4

A NEW ANOINTING

As John began his message Andy, who was already sitting on the floor, began to sink gently back into the carpet. All sense apart from the presence of God seemed to slowly fade during a delicious half hour, whilst occasional phrases and words from John's preaching confirmed what God was doing deep in Andy's spirit. It was a direct encounter with God—almost an 'out of body' experience. Afterwards Andy commented to John, 'John, that was the best message I *never* heard!'

Many have testified to similar experiences in God's presence when all else becomes as nothing compared to the sense of his closeness.

This incident marked the beginning of two wonderful days at Blaithwaite House on the outskirts of the Lake District. In September 1994, about 35 of us gathered for the inauguration of our new fellowship. Blaithwaite House Conference Centre is a favourite haunt for house parties and weekends away for many churches. It's ideally suited as a place of spiritual encounter, situated in the low-lying hills north of Keswick and south of Carlisle, nestled in the tranquillity of the Cumbrian countryside.

During the renewal, God has touched churches of all denominations and streams. It has been a wonderful time of breaking down dividing walls. For us, during the last few years our thinking on the nature of the church has been changing. We found much food for thought in the growing literature concerning the 'church at home', which sees the homes of Christian believers as the primary resource God has given for fellowship, sharing and mission. It takes as its starting point New Testament texts which speak of 'the church in your house'. Most of us, thankfully, have homes, and with open hearts and open homes much can be accomplished in the kingdom. With a group of close friends we had decided to take the step of exploring what 'home church' might be like.

However, the renewal sharpened both our thinking and experience of 'home church'. Our Blaithwaite weekend marked the beginning of a new fellowship birthed in the renewing presence of God. Celebration in the refreshing meetings at Sunderland (often with many hundreds of folk, sometimes with over a thousand) complemented the informality and spontaneity of home church in a way we were more than pleased with.

We had seen 'truth for us' in the idea of home church. Renewal added an extra dimension—home church in the power of the Spirit. In gatherings of a dozen, twenty or forty (at a squash!) in homes given to God, we have seen the Spirit move powerfully again and again.

We share our experience to help those who are from smaller churches. Sometimes, there is a fleeting thought that renewal will only be possible in the larger gatherings for celebration, at Toronto or Sunderland or in some other venue. Yet one of the great things about the present move of God is that the power of the Spirit is equally present regardless of the size of the gatherings. Indeed, the same spiritual manifestations and power have been seen when six meet in Jesus' name, as when there are 600.

A rather sophisticated, well-behaved chap . . .

Leaders in God's family come in all shapes and sizes—
every conceivable personality type. Nick is one of the
elders at SCC and provides an interesting contrast in the
leadership team. He manages his own business, is highly
educated and demonstrates a natural caution to new
things. He is married to Claire who is a pharmacist with a
large national chain. He says, 'It is amazing how the Lord
leads us according to what is best for individuals. Ken
[Gott] was happy to "jump in", but I needed the
opportunity to assess and think through what was
happening.'

God provided that opportunity and Nick and Claire,
together, sought God during a holiday teaching week –
'Focus 94'.

'Each day for a week we not only attended all the main
meetings, but also spent much time in seminars and
workshops where aspects and implications of the current
"blessing" could be addressed and discussed. It was
during this week that I became firmly convinced of the
validity and importance of what was happening.'

On returning to Sunderland, Ken and Lois Gott had
just returned from Toronto. Nick was one of the first to
receive prayer and continues his story, 'All I can say is that
something hit me and as I lay on the floor my attention
became totally absorbed by the presence of God.'

During that time God gave to Nick a vision of
marching and spreading the gospel across the whole of
the UK. What Nick was unaware of at the time was that
as he was 'seeing' the vision in the Spirit, his body was
virtually acting out what he was seeing.

'Although I was partially aware of my "real" physical
surroundings during this time, I had not realised the
extent to which my body was acting out the walking,

marching, running and stopping. This miming in response to what the Spirit is doing became not an unfamiliar feature in the days that followed.'

'When the vision concluded I found myself unable to walk, I had genuinely lost bodily strength. Then followed a scene that caused considerable amusement to a church that thought of me as a rather sophisticated, well-behaved, sensible chap. I had to be carried to our car where I was unceremoniously propped up against it while a friend got the door open. This was broad daylight, outside the church, with neighbours around and one in particular who was mesmerised by this scene as he walked his dog! This man is not drunk as you suppose—it's only two o'clock on a Sunday afternoon!'

Nick has, in the refreshing, seen a number of visions. We include just one of many:

'A few weeks into the renewal, probably early September, I was at home preparing to preach at the evening meeting. I went upstairs to get a reference book and started to read it as I came back to the top of the stairs. As I discovered that "anointed" literally meant to be "Messiah-ed" or "Christ-ed", I realised that the "anointing" we were currently experiencing was Christ coming to us by his Spirit.

'With that the power of God hit me, I fell to the floor and tumbled down the first flight of stairs. As I lay there, an image of Christ appeared in front of me. He held his arms in a welcoming way and then turned his palms towards me to show the marks. Then he said, "That's where your sin went in". The revelation that my sin really was taken by Jesus in his body on the cross came like a thunderbolt.

'I was overcome with thanksgiving, celebration and joy which kept me overwhelmed for the next hour or so. The long-term result has been a whole new understanding of my salvation and redemption which has greatly strengthened my confidence in what Jesus has done.'

That same intensity of spiritual anointing stayed with Nick night after night and even during the day at work. But as the months drew on, Nick became aware that God was doing a very deep work. He had seen other's lives affected, marriages healed, wrong attitudes put right and any manner of other good things. Now God was doing something new in his own life.

'Due to my upbringing I felt I had a "crippled personality". I was tormented by self-doubt and lack of confidence. I just knew I was not being the new creation person Christ had made me, but nothing seemed to make the really effective change that I was looking for. So as the renewal continued into its third month I became seriously worried that when it came to looking back on this refreshing, there might be plenty of funny stories to tell but, for me, not the changes I so desperately wanted.

'By November (around the fourth month) I realised that there was something about what God was doing in the meetings that was becoming more serious. The initial "party" phase had given way to the Lord dealing in deeper ways with us. Having assured us of his love, grace and acceptance he was addressing issues of behaviour and character. I actually became more and more aware of what was wrong in me than what was right. God showed me things in myself that I had never realised were there. But what was so awful was that they seemed to be getting worse!

'Then one day the Lord showed me something that helped tremendously. There had been a lot of talk about 'soaking in the Spirit', and we had all been doing it (spending time in meetings just "absorbing" God's presence like a sponge absorbs water). Another analogy that was commonly used was of rain falling on hard, dry ground in order to soften it so that weeds (things in us not of God) can be pulled up more easily: thereby ensuring the roots are also removed due to the ground being softened. When I was asking the Lord why some things in me that I was not happy with seemed to be getting worse, he simply let me see that when rain falls it not only softens the ground, but inevitably causes plants to grow, *including weeds*. So prior to the weeds being pulled out, they actually get bigger.'

What followed for Nick was some in-depth 'weeding'. Another major turning point was when he experienced the power of God even more intensely than before, giving him a new confidence, boldness and wholeness. A clear pattern emerged of experiencing the love and assurance of God, followed by an exposure of those things not of him (a fairly painful period), followed by a 'weeding out' of those things, followed by yet another new step forward in the Spirit. What Nick experienced, and expressed very clearly, is simply God's way of making us more like his Son.

A carpet I came to know so well!

God has moved powerfully in the lives of leaders of all denominations. Randy is an amiable, good humoured and extremely likable man in his fifties. Besides being chairman of a medium sized manufacturing company, an Anglican priest, an avid member of the FGBMFI[1], he directs, with his wife Dorothy, the *Northumbria Centre of Prayer for Christian Healing*. He is no stranger to the power of the Spirit.

Dorothy had been touched in a new way when Anne Watson visited Newcastle-upon-Tyne in May 1994. On their subsequent ministry trip to Zambia in June, they

[1] Full Gospel Businessmen's Fellowship International.

saw many fall under a new anointing as whole congregations were blessed, healed and delivered where they stood or fell under the power of the Spirit.

They realised something new was in the air when at the meeting of the Healing Centre in August, those who attended seemed in some way or other 'changed'. When Randy commented on how well one of the women looked she replied, 'Oh, I have been to Sunderland!' A second person questioned gave the same reply. Randy admits that he had no clue as to what they meant. Dorothy opened the meeting, which had no sooner begun than one of the women present began to laugh. When Dorothy inquired what was the matter the lady replied, 'Don't mind me, I've been to Sunderland'. Clearly, whatever 'Sunderland' was had produced a profound effect on a number of people.

Randy admits that he wanted to laugh. He desired to be full of the joy of the Lord. He was not, however, prepared for the effect of the Holy Spirit upon him when he and Dorothy subsequently made the trip to Sunderland. He reports:

'When they came to pray with me at the time of ministry I soon fell under the anointing and I cried as I lay on that carpet, which I have subsequently got to know so well. I feel I have watered every inch of it on some evening or other. The Lord started to show me all the areas in my life where repentance was needed— pride, need for position—the list seemed endless.'

Randy cried night after night through the first four weeks of September. While some laughed, others groaned and not a few jerked, Randy found himself crying each time the Spirit of God touched him. Dorothy and Randy made a trip to Toronto. Randy cried again. They returned home—more tears!

It wasn't until near the end of October that the

anointing of tears was replaced by an anointing of joy with much laughter. All at once the intensity of tears was changed for an intensity of joy. As Randy asked God what was happening, he felt God answered in this way:

'Some years ago, you got serious. You got position, you got authority, you got possessions, you got a place in the structure, you became chairman of a company and you got to need these things. Now I want to shake them all out of you.'

Randy found the various phenomena of the Spirit made it less easy to take himself too seriously or to think of himself as important. He says,

'I tend to jerk now. It reminds me that he is the important one and not me. Rather like the three knots in the Franciscan's girdle that constantly bang on the thigh to remind them of their vows of poverty, chastity and obedience, or the phylacteries which the Jews were to wear. Jesus is saying, "Remember me and not your position". I particularly jerk when preparing the elements and presiding at communion, as if he is reminding me once again that it is not my position as an Anglican priest that is important but his presence in the bread and wine.'

What do you understand by signs and wonders?

Philip is a General Practitioner in Washington (England, not DC!), of Brethren tradition. His story is full of insight. He writes:

'1994 had been a particularly hard year for our family. I had begun the year by asking God to help me grow up because I was tired of being a baby in my faith. Almost from the moment I had prayed it things started to fall to pieces! By August I was at the lowest point emotionally that I had ever been in my life and was desperate for something to change. I seemed to be getting sucked into an existence that didn't involve God very much, and certainly one in which any supernatural experience of his power in my life seemed unlikely.

'When one of my colleagues at work said he had heard that special meetings were being held at Sunderland and that God was apparently present in a "new way", I leapt at the chance of going. And so, on the Friday night of the first week of meetings I went with my friend to see what was going on. I hoped that this really was God, but all my training as a doctor told me to "be careful" and not to get involved with something that I hadn't checked out thoroughly first.

'By the end of the evening I was confused. There were things I was seeing which I couldn't understand intellectually, but which seemed to bear the hallmark and have the "feel" of God about them. There was nothing in the meeting to suggest emotional hype. We sang songs (new to me) to a backing tape. An explanation was given about being open to the manifestations we might see, but no examples were cited. The preaching was simple and not manipulative. I could see nothing to suggest demonic activity whatsoever, but I could certainly not understand why people were laughing and jerking, apparently uncontrollably.

'When an appeal was made to come forward for prayer I decided that if God was in it he could do what he wanted, however he wanted—and if he wasn't in it he was big enough to keep me safe. Having come from a church that had its origins in the Brethren denomination, going forward for prayer was not a regular event within the context of a meeting. As I stood waiting for prayer, I became distinctly unsteady on my feet. I opened my eyes because I didn't want to fall over. A minister from a church I had gone to when I was a student came and prayed with me and suddenly I found myself on the carpet.

'I made a mental check. I was not hyperventilating. I did not have a rapid heartbeat, in fact I was pleasantly relaxed. Then something quite unexpected happened—God spoke to me. The conversation ran like this:

"What do you understand by signs and wonders?" he asked.

"A sign is something that points somewhere." I answered.

"And what about a wonder?" he asked again.

"I don't know." I replied. "I don't know what a wonder is."

"A wonder is something you wonder about." he answered. And with that our discussion ended.

'From then on I decided that God could do it his way, whatever that involved. When I fell off my chair laughing a few days later I didn't bother to try to work it out—I just enjoyed it, and I think God did too!

'About two weeks later, by this time a regular attender at the nightly meetings, God explained things in a way which I immediately understood. He said two words to me, "Spiritual Amblyopia", and showed me a picture of a small boy with a squint. Occasionally I diagnose squints in children in my job as a family doctor and realise the importance of treating them. An untreated squint will eventually cause a brain to "ignore" the "lazy eye" and blindness will result in that eye. God said to me that we have two eyes with which to "see"; the eye of the intellect which is the strong eye, and the eye of the heart which is the "lazy" eye and has become weak. The eye of the heart was in danger of becoming weak to the point of losing its vision altogether, and God did not want that to happen.

'In the natural world, lazy eyes are treated, not by operating on the weak eye to make it strong, but by patching the strong eye for a time in order that the weak eye be made stronger. God was showing me that the reason there was so much that I could not understand with my intellect, but felt comfortable with in my heart, was because he was covering the eye of my intellect in order to strengthen the eye of my heart, so I could get to know him better.

'Proverbs 3:5 says, "Trust in the Lord with all your heart and lean not on your own understanding". God was wanting to teach us to trust him with our heart first and foremost and not to rely on our intellect to determine our depth of relationship with him.'

Desperation

Some leaders were in quite desperate circumstances when they entered the renewal. David had returned from the Philippine Islands in 1993, having collapsed with complete physical burnout. He had been a preacher for 28 years but says about himself, 'I thought I was finished and would never preach again—mind worn out, body worn out, nerves shattered.'

Back in the UK David began the slow road to recovery, helped by his wife and two daughters, but spiritually he knew he had a long way to go. Towards the end of the year they began to explore a new church plant in Scarborough, which God blessed, but by the end of 1994 David admits that he was, '. . . desperate for a new touch of the Holy Spirit upon my life and ministry.'

He continues: 'I had heard what was happening at Sunderland and came to see for myself. God touched my life on that first visit and I have returned many times together with my family and some of our church members. God has begun to put me together spiritually.

'I have laughed, cried, laid on the carpet . . . and the result of it all has been a deepening of my relationship with Jesus, greater love and compassion for hurting and lost souls, more understanding and love for those in our church family, and a 'sharpening' of my sensitivity when I minister to people.

'Our church is beginning to feel the impact and is experiencing a fresh wind of the Holy Spirit blowing through. We are believing for it to impact our whole area.'

Ministry and marriage restored

Brian and Wendy had been in full-time Christian service since 1977. Like so many who give their all in service, much had been taken away and by 1994 they were in a sorry state. Wendy says they were 'spiritually dry and so emotionally battered that our marriage was struggling to survive.'

They came to Sunderland upon hearing of the renewal in August 1994. Brian was so touched, knowing that God had begun to change him, he returned with his elder and his wife. Brian began to find a new liberty in preaching and in mid September made his first ever appeal for people to come forward to receive ministry. He was surprised to see the front of the church crowded, but God met with many and Brian was thrilled.

'Since then, three ladies have testified to healing and God has touched the lives of our folks. We see marriages improved, our prayer meeting doubled in numbers and we increased it from fortnightly to weekly. A deep love has developed for the Lord and we feel excited at the prospects of reaching our estate with the gospel.'

One of the marriages to be healed was Brian and Wendy's own. Wendy tells of her first visit to Sunderland:

'I came to Sunderland to seek God in a last attempt for our marriage. I was totally desperate for God to sort out my life. I received ministry, but left Sunderland feeling disappointed and frustrated—my lifestyle appeared to be in the same mess. At our church the next day, during the evening service God wonderfully met me. During worship I was only aware of Jesus and I began to cry as he moved in my life. Later I realised what he had done. He had melted the walls I had built up around my heart over the years so that I could finally forgive the hurts. My love for my husband has been more than restored—it is better now than when I married him! My love for Jesus has also been rekindled.

'He has proved that he does indeed do "more than we can ask or think" and is continuing to work in my life.'

Not all plain sailing

It would be untrue to say that all churches have received the renewal as a good thing. Some have rejected the present move out of hand as *not* of God. In some ways, that should not surprise us. In any genuine work of God there have always been detractors.

Quite simply, opposition has always been there. Arthur Wallis demonstrates that every move of God's Spirit is spoken against, often by other believers.[2] Jonathan Edwards mentions it at length in his writings. Alexander Boddy at Sunderland faced opposition from people with international reputations, such as the Baptist Graham Scroggie.[3]

That there is opposition to renewal, often by godly people, does not mean that the renewal *is not* of God. Nor, indeed, does opposition mean the move *is* of God. To suggest either would be simply overstating the case. However, we do want to give encouragement to those

---

[2] See his chapter 'A Sign Spoken Against', in *In the Day of Thy Power*, (Christian Literature Crusade: Alresford 1956), pp 25–33.
[3] See Harper, *The Twentieth Century Pentecostal Revival*, (Hodder & Stoughton: London, 1965).

who have faced opposition and misunderstanding in the renewal. For although opposition does not of itself mean that the work is of God, *if* it is then there *will* be opposition. It is unavoidable.

Some leaders have shared with us how they have dealt with opposition. One pastor writes:

'We tried to encourage people to talk and ask about all that was going on, but still a divide began to emerge. Some are simply unable to accept what is happening, even suggesting it is a work of the enemy, not the Holy Spirit. And there are those who have struggled to make up their minds about it at all.'

Despite the difficulties the same pastor summarises the move of God as on the whole very positive.

'Increasingly I have seen the fruit of what God is doing in a healing and deepening of relationships: a sense of love among God's people: a greater awareness of God's greatness and his Father heart of love: a greater readiness to participate in worship, in prayer, words, pictures: the release of long suppressed emotions, eg grief, anger, hurt, bringing healing at a deep level within.'

Some months after the renewal came to their church he was able to say, 'I sense that God is going deeper now, making us more open and clear channels through which his blessing and love can flow to the hurting and lost around us . . . It has not been a journey without struggles, questions, reservations or pain, but it seems that God has taken the initiative with us, and brought us into the flow of his Spirit. Our desire is to stay in that flow and respond to what the Father is saying and doing.'

Another pastor says, 'We have met opposition [to the renewal] which has been painful but refining. Satan has wanted to curb our love and devotion—but "many waters cannot quench love" (Song of Songs).'

Good pastors' wives!

Alice* had begun to experience God in a new way. She and her husband had touched the renewal both in Sunderland and in the fellowship they lead. They went on holiday to Canada, the highlight for Alice being their time in the Airport Vineyard, where she found the presence of God overpowering... literally. She shares her story with us.

'I got to know their carpet fairly well. I cried a lot especially over hurts which, as a good pastor's wife, I'd tried to "come to terms with" or to "forgive and forget". God poured in the oil of his Holy Spirit and the hurts were healed. I cried, also, over my arrogance in thinking I'd come to Toronto with a bowl to get blessing to take back for others, when I needed God so much myself. He certainly filled up my bowl and showed how much he loved me. How had I known him and loved him and served him for so many years without getting his love from my head to my heart?

'So much has happened since last autumn and God is still bringing about changes in me. I seem to have acquired a new "fruit" of the spirit... greed, although hunger sounds better. I'm greedily hungry for everything God has. Now I love him so much and his love and grace have affected every area of my life. My priorities are changing, my interests, free time, conversations, friendships and sleep patterns have changed too.

'I'm so excited at all God is doing in me and in all our "flock", so grateful for the "well" at Sunderland, and the opportunity to go there.'

Cathy* is another pastor's wife who was in need of refreshing. Before her visit to Sunderland she had experienced a few months of spiritual dryness. A number of people, who had previously been friends, suddenly seemed to turn away when Cathy had nothing left to give them. This resulted in a deep distrust of others, especially Christians. Cathy had become quite bitter. Even though she knew it was not right she was powerless to deal with the feelings which remained. One meeting at SCC changed that:

'It was amazing! I was prayed with and ended up on the floor. Suddenly everything lifted, all the feelings of distrust and bitterness disappeared in a moment. A few meetings later God spoke to me clearly and said, "I'm burning a love for my people in you." '

Cathy testifies that the feelings of bitterness have never returned. A few weeks later at SCC she found herself ministering to those who had caused the most hurts. Cathy summarises her experience:

'I still look back in surprise to think that feelings I had struggled with for months could disappear so quickly and so completely. Now I just want to serve God and walk in his will.'

CHAPTER 5

CARRYING THE FLAME

I want my church back

A common theme in the stories of many church leaders centres around the area of control. It was certainly Ken and Lois Gott's experience when they returned from Toronto and much blessing was released when they obeyed God.

Others have found a similar release. David is a Baptist pastor in Bishop Auckland, County Durham. He admits to some hesitation on his first visit to Sunderland, but came expressing an openness to any genuine move of the Spirit of God. He was reassured that the emphasis from the leaders was on fruit and not on the strange manifestations which were clearly evident. David was also deeply impressed by testimonies that God was restoring relationships, giving people boldness in witnessing and touching hearts at a deep level. Sunderland was indeed a safe place to be!

David encouraged his church members to see for themselves and many, including David himself, received a new and deeper touch from God. One night, God addressed the issue of 'control' in his life. David was challenged to give the church back to God, to let God do among his people what he wanted to do—to let God be God.

It was this releasing of the church that seemed to usher in a new stage in God's dealing with them. Prayer and ministry became a regular feature of their church life, with a new eagerness and expectancy among many in the fellowship. The phenomena seen at Toronto, London, and Sunderland became a part of the evening meetings in Bishop Auckland.

Renewal and growth

Alf is another pastor who shared with us that it was after 'handing the church back to God' that the church took a significant step forward. Alf, and members of his church, have been associated with the renewal at Sunderland since very near the beginning and the challenge to 'relinquish control' came in August 1994.

Allowing God to be God, to do that which he wants without undue control from leadership, seems to be a key to releasing blessing in the church. After Alf's significant step in August, Hexham Community Church became a place where laughter and tears, trembling and falling became a new norm during worship. But would it continue? Some eight months later we asked Alf for an update. He told us:

'In restoring to the Lord Jesus the executive leadership of the local church last August, we had no intimation of the exciting and faith-challenging events that were to ensue. He most certainly took us at our word!

'Soon after moving into our new premises we found ourselves pressed for space, especially on a Sunday morning. Shortly after the turn of the year we were presented with the opportunity to secure much larger accommodation above our leased premises. The rental required seemed far beyond our current means, but the Lord gave us a plan for acquisition. His scheme proved effective and since that time funds have flowed wonderfully and, together with the liberal giving of skills and labour on the part of the membership, an auditorium is being beautifully renovated to accommodate five times our present numbers. Further indication of his plans for use of the building have also been clearly communicated, much beyond our initial anticipations.

'Our Sunday services have evidenced a greater awareness of the presence and power of God. The emergence and development of prophetic ministry has been a rewarding and dynamic feature of the corporate life. In particular we have been consistently challenged to give one hundred per cent of our lives to him, especially in preparation for the harvest to come.

'As we continue to give space to the Holy Spirit's rivers of refreshment, lives have registered radical changes in response. The timid have become bold: the weak are being strengthened: callings and giftings are emerging.

'The general level of expectation is running commensurately high. His leadership is anything but dull and constricting. He has surely justified his position!'

No going back

'God wants his church back!' As Lois Gott uttered those words on Thursday August 18th 1994, Malcolm realised God was directly addressing him. Malcolm and Jayne lead an Assemblies of God church in Morpeth, Northumberland.

Malcolm confesses that in the early summer of 1994 he tried desperately to 'get away' from that which God had begun to do in many places. Strange manifestations had occurred in his own church—Malcolm had decided that they weren't going to happen again! He ministered in Tunbridge Wells only to find that Marc Du Pont from Toronto had ministered the two previous evenings. He was even asked to cover the pulpit at SCC when Ken Gott visited Holy Trinity Brompton!

Malcolm's decision to give the renewal a miss made for a fairly miserable summer. By the time the Spirit fell upon Sunderland Malcolm says, 'I was about ready to pack in.'

On his Thursday visit to Sunderland Malcolm found himself in the front row, very apprehensive, but, ' . . . like all leaders desperately trying to show that I had it all together.' He continues his story:

'During the worship God began to open me up bit by bit. I was even beginning to enjoy it, although when we started to worship along with a tape I thought it a little strange![1] Then came those words "God wants his church back". It was as if someone stood in front of me and pushed me in the chest. I ended up in a heap in the row behind, but quickly formulated a prayer to the effect, "Lord, if you're going to be this violent about it, have your church back".'

The following Sunday, during a baptism service, Malcolm made a public statement to the church. He was just about to call people forward for prayer when he felt God say, 'Don't you dare do this until you repent of not allowing me the room I have wanted in this church.'

Malcolm had learnt to be obedient, and so he apologised to the congregation. They graciously accepted and he proceeded to pray with people.

'As I prayed for the first person, I extended my hand towards him. As I did so he fell to the ground—and so did I! All I wanted to do was get up and lay hands on as many people as I could. Within ten minutes between forty and fifty people were on the floor meeting God in ways they

---

[1] At the beginning of the renewal use was made of 'live worship' tapes from the Vineyard Ministries International which contained a number of new songs which had arisen out of the refreshing. As soon as music was available, live bands were used!

had never done before. We have not been the same since that day.'

The renewal has continued ever since. Malcolm comments on the fruit of renewal in the church:

'Many people "on the fringe" last year are now committed to pursuing all that God has for them. The sense of God in our meetings is such that there have been times when some of us have felt that revival could break out there and then. We have more prayer meetings than we have ever had, a hunger for the word like never before, and a desire to serve God which is so strong that we are constantly looking for ways to release people into ministry.'

Malcolm is also aware of a deepening of his own walk with God. 'He . . . exposed a lot of personal ambition in my heart, a desire to please and be seen and recognised by men. To realise that you're popular with God, even if you aren't always popular with men, is a very releasing thing.'

With others, Malcolm and Jayne have also faced difficulties in the refreshing. 'The Holy Spirit has "stirred the waters" in all of our lives. We haven't always liked what we've seen either in our lives or in the lives of others. But he's done that for a purpose—to change us degree by degree into the likeness of his Son.

'We never want to go back to where we once were, even if we knew the way.'

Malcolm, Jayne and members of their church are frequently seen at the renewal meetings. 'Drinking at the well' is an ongoing and important part of their lives.

It's my ministry not yours

Many leaders face the danger of taking the whole burden of the ministry upon themselves. In the end it always produces frustration, dryness and leads relentlessly towards 'burnout'.

Paul had realised all of that. When he came to Sunderland it was with a desire to know God in a deeper way—Paul had simply become dissatisfied with his Christian life. As he was approached for prayer he began to tell how he was feeling, how dry and barren he was, how passion for the ministry had gone and yet of his deep desire to give more of himself to God and to receive all that God had for him. Paul shared his experience,

'The next thing I remember was lying face down on the carpet, very still and relaxed. I could hear what was happening around me, but I had no interest in it. I just wanted to seize my moment with God, and my moment came. "Paul", the Holy Spirit said, "It's my ministry, it's not your ministry". I wept and pleaded with God to take it from me. I could see I was carrying burdens which were not mine to carry, and taking credit for that which I had no right to take credit for. I was just full of repentance: "O God forgive me, I'm so sorry, please have it back, it doesn't belong to me, it's yours Jesus—all the glory is yours."

'After several minutes of this the Holy Spirit spoke again, "But I've chosen to bless you with it." Upon hearing this I felt such joy I thought I would burst! And that's exactly what I did. I laughed and cried together. "God you want to use me? You want to bless my life? O God, thank you, thank you!" '

The fire of God In Northern Ireland

It has often been said that Sunderland is a place to come and receive and then to take that which has been received back to one's own fellowship. Hence, once a month an afternoon is specifically arranged for those who are in leadership to come and meet with each other and with God. Usually about 200–300 gather: some are from the local area, others from much further afield. It has been good to meet others from many denominations and to declare that our denominational differences no longer matter. Through the meetings many have been affected and have gone back to their fellowships refreshed and later have given testimony that their whole church has found God in a new way.'

In the early autumn of 1994 Crawford and Joan received a telephone call. An excited voice said, 'You have to come over here and see what God is doing in our meetings.'

It was from their good friend, Diane, who is a member of the local fellowship at SCC. She told them a little of what had happened to Ken and Lois and what was happening throughout the church. It whetted their appetite sufficiently for them to arrange to visit the next weekend. So it was that at 11.30 pm on the following Friday, Crawford and Joan arrived from County Antrim, Northern Ireland. They found it strange that first weekend. It was a completely new experience to see the manifestations and most of the time they observed from the back of the hall. However, before they left to catch the ferry they asked Ken Gott to pray with them and on the way home they talked about all they had seen and heard. Crawford says,

'We realised we should have entered in and received what God had for us. Being at those services gave us a hunger for more of the things of God. We couldn't wait to get back again to SCC.'

Crawford and Joan next came to Sunderland in October 1994 for the first visit of John and Carol Arnott. Both evenings over a thousand people gathered, the biggest crowd ever in the SCC building. Crawford tells us his experience of it:

'The church was packed out and the presence of the

Lord was mighty. The worship was really anointed and several people were falling off their feet with the presence of God. My wife and I couldn't wait for the ministry time to start. We were hungry for more of God. Well, God didn't disappoint us and we were on the carpet for over an hour just receiving from the Lord.'

Crawford felt he should ask his pastor friend David to accompany him to the next leaders' meeting at Sunderland. Crawford was amazed at the reply he received when he telephoned David.

'You won't believe this, Sally [his wife] and I are sitting here talking about the "Toronto blessing". She said to me "David you will have to go somewhere to find out more about it". The next thing the 'phone rang and you ask me to go to Sunderland. Crawford, this 'phone call is a divine appointment, I want to go with you.'

Crawford and David made the now familiar journey to the North-East of England. They both received a lot from God, Crawford continues with his account:

'I could feel the presence and the power of the Lord going right through my body. I could feel my hands burning hot and a tingling feeling coming through them. I was concerned about David, but unknown to me several minutes after I fell down David had also fallen under the anointing, so the Lord really touched us that evening.'

Crawford and David returned again to Sunderland. Crawford was prayed over with the words, 'Lord release the fire of God in his belly'.

Crawford felt his hands and arms shaking, his whole body felt as if it were on fire. He continued to be prayed for and to receive right through that meeting and into the evening meeting. The effect on his life was enormous. When he arrived home he couldn't wait to lay hands on the folks in his church. On Sunday mornings Crawford's church has a time of prayer before the service begins. The room was quite full that morning and he had to brush past his pastor. Instantly the pastor started to praise God and pray. He told Crawford that he had felt the power of God on him from the moment of Crawford's accidental touch. Later that week Crawford shared at the prayer meeting. Again he was powerfully anointed as he spoke and as he prayed with many of the people they, too, received the power of God and as Crawford says 'Things are starting to happen in our church.'

Crawford concludes by saying, 'The meetings in SCC have given me a desire for more of the things of God in my life. I would like to say that Joan and myself really appreciate SCC and all the friends we have made there. We will continue to come back for more of God and hope to bring many more people with us to receive what God is doing there.'

Industrial revolution—spiritual revolution

Like Sunderland, Telford in Shropshire is a birthplace of industry. It was one of those places which during the Industrial Revolution became a centre of growth and phenomenal change. Telford was also the place of John Fletcher's labours in the eighteenth century when a well of spiritual blessing was established.

In 1994–1995 there were prophecies that Telford would become a place of spiritual revolution. September 1994 saw the beginning of monthly renewal meetings with an attendance of around 120. By May 1995 numbers had increased to between 250 and 300 and a renewal conference with 450 delegates. God is moving powerfully again in Telford.

Trevor and Sharon are leaders at Springfield Christian Fellowship in Telford. They were challenged to start holding the renewal meetings whilst in Sunderland for a visit, just after Christmas. Sharon relates how God spoke to them:

'Trev was lying on the floor and heard God ask him, "Do you want one of these?". Before he could answer the reply came, "Because I have plenty of them!" '

A week later they viewed a local factory unit and started negotiations to rent the property. At the time of writing they have had the keys for a week and are looking forward to their first renewal meeting on the new premises. They are expecting God to do great things. They tell us:

'We have furnished the centre for 500 people, but it has a capacity for 750. Another church has begun the process of merging with our church. God is indeed breaking down dividing walls. The two sets of leaders could not easily enjoy each others' company, but we have been working together and relating to one another closely since September 1994 with great mutual respect.'

On a personal note Trevor, Sharon and their two daughters have been enjoying the 'refreshing' since the end of August. They first heard about what was happening on a cassette recording and subsequently visited Toronto and Sunderland. The whole family has been greatly blessed individually. Trevor tells us how they describe it to their girls:

'We are explaining to them that the essence of this move of God is changed hearts and changed lives and this is most evident in our home situation. The acid test of our walk with God is our private life.'

The fire spreads

Quite clearly, then, one of the characteristics of the present renewal has been the way that the 'fire' has been caught, carried to another place and many others in their turn set alight for God. Thousands of churches around the world now tell the story of someone from their midst visiting a place of blessing and bringing the blessing home. Sunderland has been one such place where many have received and carried God's love away with them.

It has also been the delightful experience of those who are part of the renewal at Sunderland to be used by God when they visit other places.

Frankie and Elaine visited Frankie's sister and husband in Wiltshire. At first, over the telephone, reception was, to say the least, cool. However, by the time of the visit the temperature had warmed! Frankie and Elaine were asked to speak at church that Sunday to share for about ten minutes. They spoke for fifteen minutes each, accompanied by many manifestations—jerkings, groanings, shaking, 'bobbing up and down'— Elaine says, 'looking an absolute disaster'. But the Spirit touched the congregation. People fell off chairs, others lay laughing, some sobbed. The wonder of it was that these people had never seen or experienced the Holy Spirit in that way before. It was not a learned experience or an imitation. God 'showed up' as he has in thousands of churches over the last year. Elaine and Frankie were deeply humbled as they were asked to pray for the pastor of the church and his elders.

It strikes us that humbling often takes place in those who enter the refreshing. The outward and visible manifestations are used by God as a way of 'taking people off pedestals'. Sometimes the effects can look amusing, even bizarre. It humbles leaders who have been used to delivering eloquent sermons to find themselves stumbling and stuttering over a few simple words. Those who have been proud of their personal bearing and appearance are humbled to find a manifestation of the Spirit which seems to give them the appearance of a nervous twitch!

One dear lady wrote to thank Ken Gott and Andy for ministry at an Anglican meeting in Bridlington on the Yorkshire coast. She wrote,

' . . . when Ken and Andy were on the stage talking and jerking, I felt very remote and out of it.' She had only recently suffered the loss of her father and had just returned from his burial. 'And then suddenly I couldn't help laughing at the hilarity of these two dear men being willing to be made so ridiculous in order to be living examples of God's sense of humour. Their humility and grace were so thrilling and comforting to me and my daughter of nine and I received a wonderful blessing later. I now feel so excited and full of joy at what God is doing'.

Grace is given in the humbling of God's people.

Blessing in Slovakia

Andrew and Michelle had been in the renewal since its beginning in August 1994 and had spent many hours soaking in the presence of God. Like Elaine and Frankie, they had opportunity to take God's blessing with them. Andrew reported:

'Our trip to Slovakia took place in December, and the Lord provided the funds for Michelle to accompany me. I took part in an economic development conference at the University in Banska' Bystrica, a regional administrative centre in the middle of this new nation state (formerly part of Czechoslovakia). We also took the opportunity to visit friends in ministry in that town and other places on route . . . and we had the joy of praying with them to receive God's fresh blessing.

'Again, with little background knowledge of what had been happening elsewhere, we saw a remarkable working of the Holy Spirit releasing joy and laughter, tears and repentance, prophecy and visions. Our friends had expected us to do some counselling, as on previous occasions, and seemed surprised at our change of tactics, preferring to make room for God himself to speak into the needs. But God was faithful, and one of the great joys was to receive reports after our return home, not only of the fruit in those we prayed with, but also in lifting the burden of expectation on leaders always to have the answers to every need.'

CHAPTER 6

TO HEAL THE BROKENHEARTED

There have been deep healings for many during the refreshing. We have discovered that the outward manifestation is often merely a pointer or a clue to the work God is doing deep inside. Many of these deep touches of God are, by their very nature, intensely personal. It is sometimes sad that in the media much attention has been focused on the outward things. Even in much of the Christian press discussion has, more often than not, been about that which can be seen. Of course, that's understandable as the outward is easier to see and to speak of. Those who have remained as onlookers sometimes wonder what spiritual benefit can possibly be associated with the phenomena they observe with their eyes. We include some testimonies here of the deep inner healing work which God has accomplished, often in a brief time. It seems, in the intensity of the Spirit's move, much can happen in the briefest of time spans. Some of these stories are recorded here for the first time, due to their sensitive nature. As one lady testified, 'What counsellors have tried to do in ten years, God has done in six weeks!'

Difficult times will always come, given the nature of the world we live in. God's people are not freed from the same life circumstances that others face. The difference is that a faith newly ignited by God can make all the difference in the world to the way in which we face life.

Janette had rested in God's presence many times. Her husband Ken told us:

'Janette received a fresh revelation of the love of God for her. God's timing was just right, for after having been blessed by the Holy Spirit she was diagnosed as having breast cancer. Now we know that the mention of that disease brings anxiety and fear to one's heart. But those two feelings were nonexistent and instead, because she had received this special filling of the Holy Spirit, that 'peace which passes all understanding' was her portion. Even the operation had no fear for her and, thank God, the tumour was removed and the surgeon's report was "no cancer now in the breast". Oh, how we thank God for his Holy Spirit for such a time as this.'

Abused and healed

One of the astonishing and repeated occurrences in the renewal is the sheer speed with which God moves in people's lives. We have no wish to denigrate much counselling which frequently takes place in the church. Nor are we suggesting that this renewal is a 'quick fix'. It does seem, however, that in the presence of God that which often takes many, many hours to discern and talk through, God can perform in a brief time. We are making an observation from listening to the testimonies of many. God is healing, bringing to maturity and moving very quickly in the lives of those who have been touched.

Janet* told us of deep hurts from a terribly abusing situation which had affected her relationships with men for many years:

'As a nineteen-year-old I fell very much in love with a Norwegian student, eight years my senior. He was very romantic and attentive and made me feel precious to him.

We became engaged to be married and I could not have felt happier. During the summer vacation I gave up my job and went to Norway to meet his family and find a home ready for the following spring when we intended to marry.

'During the two months spent there I worked as an *au pair* near to his home and all was well, I thought. I soon realised, however, that I had made a terrible mistake. He became very possessive and wanted to know what I had been doing every minute of the day. He would become extremely angry if my employers decided to have a night out or have me go somewhere with them, without letting him know first. His outbursts of temper would frighten me, but I convinced myself it was because he loved me. I soon discovered, however, that he saw me as his private property and heaven help anyone (including me) who said otherwise. As I began to withdraw from him emotionally and resist his control, his temper turned to violence resulting in my being beaten and raped.

'I felt trapped. I was in a foreign country, no relatives or friends, and no money to return home. I was deeply ashamed to find myself in this situation and did not want anyone to know, so I kept quiet and took his now regular beatings and abuse while trying to work out how to get out of the situation. The only way I could hold on to any self-esteem was to put up a fight each time, which made him even angrier and I seemed caught in a vicious circle.

'Fortunately, my employer noticed the change in me (there were never any marks or bruises to be seen) and that I was unhappy. She offered me my fare home, saying I could repay it once I got a job back in England, which I did immediately. I made the excuse to my fiancé that I was homesick. He was not happy but was reassured by my pretending that I would see him when he came back to England. I then wrote from England to break off our engagement, feeling safe once more at home.

'I would like to say that was the end, but what followed was weeks of threatening phone calls, threats to kill me. He decided that if he could not have me, no one else could. I was so angry by this time I told him to go ahead with his threats—I didn't really care anymore. I never heard from him again.

'Fourteen years later as a married woman with two children I met Jesus, the One who gives unconditional love. I became aware that my past held things I had to face and deal with through the love and help of the Holy Spirit. I saw I needed to forgive my ex-fiancé and pray for him, which I did. I then needed to forgive myself. I had always blamed myself and carried the responsibility and guilt for what had happened. It seemed harder to forgive myself than it had been to forgive him. The next thing the Lord showed me was that my dislike of women's company was because I looked down on myself and transferred that to other women. As I repented of that he gave me a great love for my sisters in Christ and led me into a women's ministry. All this happened in the first three to four years of my walk with the Lord and I thought it was all dealt with.

'However, in the time of refreshing and moving of the Spirit I was lying on the carpet at SCC one night when I began to weep uncontrollably. The cry deep in my heart was to be able to relate to the men of the church as my brothers, as Christ intended, without an ounce of fear and without feeling the need to keep the walls of defence up in an effort to protect myself. The Lord showed me that because the violence and abuse had come from someone whom I had loved and who I thought had loved me, I was withholding God's love for fear of being vulnerable again and of being misunderstood and giving out wrong signals to the opposite sex. He wanted me free to love men and women equally and to be a blessing to my brothers as well as my sisters in the Lord.

'I know that night in SCC God changed my fear into his love and it is something that I am growing into and my brothers are truly my brothers with a purity which I never thought I could experience. I look at them and share with them and know there is no longer a shadow there from the past—I am free! Hallelujah, his perfect love casts out all fear!

'As if to confirm what the Lord was doing, the following Sunday, one of the men in my church walked up to me, gave me a hug and said, "We need more sisters like you in the church." That precious word "sister" was like being given a handful of jewels. I trust and pray that God will continue to release women like myself who have been held back by low self-esteem brought about by past experiences.'

Sheila* was rejected as a child and raped at sixteen. She hated her mother. She was illiterate and turned to gambling and smoking. As she had never experienced love as a child she, in turn, found it difficult to care for her own family. Everything changed on June 5th 1988. That was the day she became a Christian. Sheila testifies, 'From the day I gave my heart to the Lord he started to mould me and soften my heart.'

Sheila found that she was free from her addictions and was able to learn to read and write. . . a marvellous thing for her. The whole family, all now Christians, entered the refreshing in August 1994. Sheila found that all that God was doing suddenly took on a new intensity. As she lay in God's presence over the ensuing months, she felt God healing her:

'I felt like the Lord was squeezing me, putting his arms around me, squeezing everything out: then putting new in. [He's] put love in, taken hatred, hardness and hurting off me.

'Times have still been hard, but the last six months have been great'.

Prayer partners

Sue heard about the blessing at the beginning of September and decided to go to Sunderland to see what was happening. She found it a very noisy night with lots of laughter, but Sue was quick to receive prayer in the ministry time. Equally quickly she found herself on the floor!

'After about ten minutes I began to think about getting up, but discovered that I was literally pinned to the floor. God told me to "rest in him" and kept me there for over an hour. I got up feeling more refreshed than I had in years.'

That was the first of many trips to Sunderland and God has continued to meet her:

'Over the past six months God has shown me how much he loves me and has given me a new, increased love for him and also for others. He has also restored broken relationships with other Christians, healed past hurts and released from the bonds of unforgiveness.

'I have always felt a responsibility for my family's spiritual lives but I was shown early on that, although I had a responsibility to lift them in prayer, the burden was God's, not mine, and it was more important to get my own relationship with him in order. Having been released from the burden, I began to see how shallow my own relationship had been and this is gradually being dealt with.'

Another longing of Sue's heart was for a prayer partner. God answered this one weekend at SCC when Sue responded to an altar call asking for any who felt they were called to be intercessors. Sue found herself following Annie out. The two live in the same Northumberland town and worship in the same 'home church' network, although in different groups. Since that evening they have met for prayer and intercession each week.

Annie has also shared her story with us. Her first visit to Sunderland was with her husband and some friends from Oxford. Over the months God has done some powerful and deeply personal things with Annie. Some of the things are too deep and too personal to share publicly, however there were parts of her story that Annie told us:

'[When] I was thirteen years old three of my friends were killed over a succession of two years. These accidents were horrific and left me emotionally scarred. I was totally unable to express "deep emotion" especially in public. At that time I went "off the rails" and started drinking and taking drugs.

'Until recently I had not connected all this with being unable to express emotion. One night, while doing "carpet time", someone very special and safe to me started praying that God would give me a gift of tears. For two hours solidly I cried in public, without shame, without guilt and totally free.'

God has continued to release Annie. We tell one other incident which happened just recently:

'God released my "creativity". The last thing my best friend Joyce and I did together at school, before she was killed, was a painting. I have never been able to paint, to draw or do anything artistic since—even singing, which I love, was deeply hidden. God has given me a freedom to paint, to dance and to run in his presence.'

Knowing God as Father

David* is from South Wales, having been brought up in a small mining community. He became more or less independent by the age of fourteen and can't remember ever being hugged, kissed or told he was loved by his parents. At the age of seventeen he joined the army, where he remained for the next twenty-two years. David remembers the day he left to join. 'My mother never even got out of bed to see me off.'

In the army David survived by building walls and hiding the real him. As he says, 'At least that way there was little chance of being emotionally hurt. I stuck to this practice for many years and have really only let my wife and children see the real me, and even then only on the odd occasion.'

In the refreshing God has been changing David's heart towards the people who had hurt him in the past. David recalls one evening during the ministry time:

'God burdened my heart with a need to contact my father and tell him I loved him. This was something that I could never remember telling him, and until that day had no intention or inclination to do so.

'Later that day I did 'phone my dad and told him I loved him. I felt a tremendous weight had been lifted off me, which I believe was guilt for not having expressed my love to my parents. Also I forgave them for not demonstrating their love for me.'

David found he also forgave acquaintances from his time in the army whom he believed had wronged him. He knows only God enabled him to do this: 'It's only by God's grace and love towards me that I have been able to let go of the bitterness in my heart towards them.'

Joan had heard about the meetings in Sunderland and had determined not to go. However, she had a friend who wished to go and needed a lift. Without Joan's car her friend would be unable to stay for the whole meeting. Joan sat through the meeting and stood at the back during the ministry time. The second time she took her friend and again stood at the back, but this time an old friend asked if she wanted prayer. Joan declined, the friend persisted. 'Joan, you're dry and thirsty and barren. You're dying.'

Joan almost ran from the building, but whilst driving home God spoke to her. She felt God told her that she was dry, thirsty, barren and dying. When she arrived home Joan wept before God, confessing her criticism and blindness. Later as the tears ceased, a wonderful sense of peace invaded her room.

Joan returned to Sunderland on many occasions but in ministry time was frightened. Her fear was that secret, habitual sins would be revealed. However, God showed her that he knew all about her and still loved her with a passion. She says,

'My love went from being something very ordinary to something so special and real and precious that my life had to become "holy to God".'

Some weeks later God showed her a picture. She wasn't sure what God was saying in it, but it left her sobbing brokenheartedly. However, the next night, unbeknown to him, Ken Gott said in his preaching what God was revealing to Joan in her vision. As God showed her that she must realise a spirit of adoption, Joan remembered the abuse she had suffered at the hand of her father. She tells us:

'As I forgave my natural father, so God allowed me to feel his acceptance of me. Before I knew in my head that God would not ignore me, now I know in my heart. I am accepted at the Father's side, not because I am anyone, but because Christ is his Son.

'God is such a huge God and all he has is to bless me.'

Mark* also needed to find God as Father. He had reached a very low ebb by summer 1994.

'My most frequent prayer was for God to give up on me and destroy my existence. I was simply unable to accept a loving father-like God who could give so abundantly and deeply.

'After many years, living with the emotional mess of a very unhappy childhood, God began a deep release and healing. It seemed as if he knew precisely what to touch to bring that release and his touch was not harsh.'

Mark cried that night, a deep sobbing, which was the beginning of a real sense of freedom. Then God started to fill Mark.

'As he [God] washed away the hurt and the fear, then I began to receive his filling. Many times God has told me of his love for me, how much I am accepted and precious, one of his sons, a child that would become really adopted in his family.

'I am learning that a living, active relationship of being freed, restored, loved and guided even in the small details is the power to living as a Christian. I am discovering that God does not abandon me, that serving him is a blessing and that he is always willing to give much more of himself to me. Now I can say that I do love God as Father.'

Pouring out his healing love

Christine is a widow with three teenage children. She felt that she was continually being torn in two. Every decision was a problem to her, 'Should I go out or stay in? Should I play the guitar or not? Should I go to church or not?'

She knew that her indecision was rooted in fear. Many years of counselling had helped only a little, although as she says, 'I am so grateful for the people God placed me with who loved me and still do.'

Then Christine visited Sunderland and was ministered to.

'When God began to pour out his Spirit in incredible measure, I felt him saying to me "There's been enough talking and trying to work things out. I'm coming myself. I'll do it."

'As I kept coming to him, coming meeting after meeting, he poured out his healing love.'

Christine cried 'buckets of tears' for the next ten weeks and then she knew that God had healed her. She testifies to it:

'I was on the floor, out in the Spirit, and I just knew that he had healed my mind and my personality, he'd healed the split. I suddenly had one mind, one heart, one soul, one personality. . . it was incredible and I hadn't even asked!'

Christine admits that there is still a lot more healing needed in her life, but is confident that as God continues to pour out his love, she will continue to have the past hurts healed.

Mary also needed to have past hurts healed. Ten years previously her sixteen-year-old son was killed in a road accident. Over the years God had been gradually healing her, especially from the grief that overwhelmed her whenever she heard an ambulance. She tells us what the last few months have meant to her:

'In this latest move of God's spirit he has healed me from grief which I must have suppressed when we left James [her son] in ITU, knowing he was brain dead, but he was still on a ventilator. The Lord has ways of bringing up past hurts which we think we have already dealt with, which he needs to heal by the power of the Spirit.'

Over the weeks Mary felt she had also been healed of memories from when she was in primary school. There she felt hurt and humiliated by her low marks, as she was made to stand up in class and admit to them. God showed her that his love was not dependent on her performance. She concludes her account:

'I have a greater love for Jesus, and it is exciting wondering what God is going to do each day. The shaking and the jerking which I am experiencing at the moment is, I think, God's way of dealing with my self-conciousness. Also I feel that he is increasing my faith and burdening me for intercessory prayer.

Three years in a wheelchair—released

Jan and Joe live in Sunderland where they are members of the local Baptist church. April 1995 is a month they will never forget! Jan had been ill for the preceding twenty-three years, becoming progressively more disabled with an undiagnosable illness. For the last three years she had been in a wheelchair, unable to walk, unable to dress herself and even unable to feed herself. Joe did all the cooking and cared for their three children.

They had been to a few renewal meetings, and enjoyed the presence of God. Then at a meeting in April during the worship time Jan felt a tingling through her body. She says, 'It was like electricity all through me.'

Joe went to receive ministry. He couldn't believe it when, at the close of the meeting, he found his wife. She told him, 'I've stood and walked a few steps.'

We saw them a week later in the renewal meeting. Andy called Jan forward to testify—amazed at seeing her walk into the auditorium sporting a new pair of court shoes!

A month later we asked for an update. There is no trace

of the former illness. Jan is a very active young woman. She says:

'I've never looked back. It's even a pleasure to wash up after not being able to do the dishes for so long! Last week we asked social services to come and take the stair lift out. They were astonished at the request . . . apparently it normally only happens when someone dies!'

Her family are equally amazed. Her eleven-year-old daughter told us, 'It's absolutely amazing. God's really done something for Mum.'

Duncan and Paul, her sons, said, 'All right! Magnificent! Really brilliant!'

Husband Joe says, 'It's wonderful. I've never been in love with Jesus like I am now.'

We have included only a small sample of the many deep works of healing we have seen in the Sunderland renewal. We thank God for them all, whether inner or physical healing, often both, and pray that there will be many more. All glory be to God!

CHAPTER 7

A LITTLE CHILD SHALL
LEAD THEM

On most evenings during the renewal, after the message from the Scriptures, chairs are moved in order to provide space for people to be prayed with. One night in late September, as usual, all who wished to be prayed for were invited to stand and move into a space. On this occasion our daughter, Rebekah, then aged ten, and her twelve-year-old friend, Jenny, stood near to the front. They were eager to be touched by God and as each was prayed with in turn, God met them in a very special way. The two little girls lay side by side under the power of the Spirit for nearly two hours. Rebekah later described it as 'laughing, crying, shaking and being peaceful.' Many of the ministry team took turns to stay with the girls and pray for them, in their turn receiving blessing from God as they entered the anointing which was very apparent on the two children.

Afterwards we asked Rebekah if God had spoken to her. 'He showed me a picture', she said, 'It was a big white hand holding the world in it.'

Her friend, Jenny, joined us. We asked her if God had shown her anything. 'Yes', she replied, 'I saw God's hand with a white light shining on it and it was holding the world.'

Those of us who listened were amazed, for, although

expressed slightly differently, the girls had obviously seen the same picture and we knew that there had not been any opportunity for them to speak with each other. It was another confirmation for Jane (Andy was at that time in the States, and amazed at the report over the telephone) that we were beginning to experience something very special from God.

Children in the history of renewal

In every period of spiritual awakening children have been deeply affected. John Wesley noted on a number of occasions that in periods of renewal children receive deeply from God, sometimes before the adults and more than once were used to bring the grown-ups into renewal. He speaks of children being 'much affected' and 'crying out', then falling to their knees confessing the Saviour.[1] He recorded on Monday 6th September 1773

> Presently the Spirit fell upon them [the children], and then the Spirit of grace and supplication, till the greater part of them were crying together for mercy, with a loud and bitter cry . . . all but one (two-and-twenty in number) were exceedingly comforted.

He commented a week later after observing more of God's work among the children:

> I suppose such a visitation of children has not been known in England these hundred years. In so marvellous a manner, 'out of the mouths of babes and sucklings' God has 'perfected praise'!

---

[1] See, for instance his journal entry dated Friday September 3rd 1773, in *The Journal of John Wesley*, (Standard Edition), Ed. Nehemiah Curnock, (Epworth Press: London, 1938).

Some years later, whilst visiting Stockton-on-Tees, Wesley found that the work of God began with the children. Around sixty came to receive instruction from him. The Spirit came upon them and the children all fell to their knees. Wesley knelt with them. Adults who observed this called others until many older people joined with the children upon whom the Spirit had fallen. He comments:

> The fire kindled and ran from heart to heart, till few, if any, were unaffected. Is not this a new thing in the earth? God begins his work in children. Thus it has been in Cornwall, Manchester, and Epworth. Thus the flame spread to those of riper years, till at length they all know Him from the least unto the greatest.[2]

There have been other instances of children leading adults to Christ. In 1859 on the east Coast of Scotland it was reported in the local press that:

> A boy of 8 years of age once, under strong convictions, spoke in the meeting, and his words made such a deep impression that more were convicted and converted than on any other occasion. He still continues to speak, but not with his former power.[3]

Jonathan Edwards, similarly, observed in the revivals in New England that:

> Very many little children have been remarkably enlightened, and their hearts wonderfully affected and enlarged, and their mouths opened, expressing themselves in a

---

[2] Tuesday 8th June, 1784 in the *Journal*.
[3] Quoted in Harry Sprange, *Kingdom Kids, The Story of Scotland's Children in Revival*, (Christian Focus Publications: Fearn, 1994), p 184. Sprange's treatment of children in revival in Scotland is both exhaustive and enlightening and worth reading by anyone interested in God and children.

manner far beyond their years, and to the just astonishment of those which have heard them.[4]

By the same token, in the revivals in other parts during the eighteenth century children were a part of the great move of God. As the Spirit was poured out children were 'awakened' (sometimes with a limited meaning of becoming aware of their sin, sometimes with the broader understanding of full conversion), some saw visions, many were moved to tears and some were affected with the bodily phenomena we have seen in abundance in the present renewal. For example, in the revival at Kilsyth, Scotland

> There were half a dozen boys, in whom also convulsive motions appeared to come to a greater height, and to make them insensible for some time . . .[5]

Common in the periods of revival are children who come to a deep knowledge of God's love for them personally, turning them to prayer and a true walk of faith. Sometimes there is a thought that children should not be expected to believe, that they should be left until they are adults to make a mature and considered commitment of their own. On the contrary, in the renewal at Sunderland we have found that even in quite small children there can be a great sense of the divine. Robert Murray McCheyne commented that in the revival of 1839 ministers treated children in the same way as adults, with remarkable success. He commented:

> The ministers . . . have . . . spoken to children as freely as to grown persons: and God has so greatly honoured their

---

[4] *Thoughts on the Revival*, p 375.
[5] James Robe, minister in Kilsyth from 1713 who saw revival in 1742, in Sprange, *op cit*, p 31

labours that many children from ten years old and upwards, have given full evidence of their being born again . . . It was commonly at public meetings . . . that children were impressed, often also in their own little meetings, when no minister was present.[6]

There were many instances of children 'prostrated' during the general revival of 1859. It is, however, somewhat difficult to get through to exactly what happened because each recalling of the phenomena is accompanied by an interpretative commentary. Those who believed the experience to be of God couched the 'prostration', 'swooning' or 'convulsion' in terms of the awareness of sin and conviction by God. Those who commented in a negative fashion spoke of 'transports of religious delirium', 'frantic gestures' and 'swaying . . . bodies backwards and forwards'.[7] It seems fairly clear, though, that what was being described was a fair approximation of what we are seeing at present amongst children night after night.

Little ones touched

From the beginning of the renewal at Sunderland we believed that God was going to do something very special with the pre-teens. It was deeply moving to see how eagerly the little children wanted to be in the meetings and to be prayed for. It was humbling to see their simple, yet profound faith reach out to Jesus and for the Spirit to be received easily and readily as these precious little ones lay in his presence. The look of sheer pleasure and peace on the faces of children affected by the Spirit is one we shall not easily forget!

---

[6] A. Bonar, *Memoirs and Remains of Rev. Robert Murray McCheyne*, 1892, p 547, in Sprange, *op cit*, p 57.

[7] See Sprange, *op cit*, pp 118–119.

Jesus, himself, had emphasised the importance of little children. He had taken aside a child and said 'Whoever becomes humble like this child is the greatest in the kingdom of heaven' and, again 'Let the little children come to me, and do not stop them: for it is to such as these that the kingdom of heaven belongs.' Listening to the children tell us their stories it has impressed us how unselfconscious they are. It is not surprising that immediately after Jesus has spoken those words (Mt 19:14), he is approached by the rich young man asking what good deed he could do to earn eternal life. The contrast between him and the little child is startling. In his reply Jesus shows the young man that he is cluttered up with his religious teachings and with his possessions. Unfortunately, in his adult complexity and sophistication, he can't find the simplicity of the children and he remains disappointed and dejected when he leaves Jesus.

Another example of a child being greatly used by God is Samuel. I Samuel 3 tells us that the word of the Lord was rare in those days. Yet when God wanted to speak he chose to do it through a little boy who had 'grown in favour with the Lord'. In this time of refreshing we have tried to ensure that little children have not been marginalised or seen as less likely to hear from God. Actually they have been shown wonderful simple truths of God, often through pictures and they, too, have fallen in love with Jesus in a deeper way. They have become evangelists within their schools, unashamedly telling their friends and teachers about all the things they have seen and heard as God has wonderfully touched their young lives.

Children and prophecies

There have, in recent years, been prophetic voices raised in this direction. Jean Darnell, in her now famous vision of a coming revival, spoke of a number of signs of the coming awakening. The second sign she speaks of is that of a new revelation of Jesus to children. She says:

> . . . the Lord is going to send a tremendous revelation of Himself to boys and girls in this country. Between the ages of nine and fifteen particularly, children will begin to see a revelation of Jesus. They will see Him, they will know Him, they will hear Him, He will speak to them. He will come to them in visions and dreams, He will reveal His word to them. They will be converted and filled with the Holy Spirit and gifted by Him.[8]

We have certainly observed an intensification of all these things amongst children who have experienced the renewal. The vision continues:

> . . . their experiences will be real. Some of their experiences will be so unusual you may doubt them. At that point receive their testimonies at face value, give them the word of God, and teach them how to love: because these children will have ministries not only as children, but as leaders in their adult life, and they will bless this country and other countries.

Similarly, Rick Joyner in his record of prophecies given in 1987 and 1988, says, of the coming awakening:

> Teenagers will be the backbone of the revival, and pre–teens will be some of its greatest evangelists. Young children will cast out demons, heal the sick, raise the dead, and divert raging floods with a word.[9]

---

[8] For a full transcript of the prophecy see Hugh Black, *Revival*, (New Dawn Books: Greenock, 1993), pp 103–122.

[9] Rick Joyner, *The Harvest*, (Whittaker House: Springdale, 1989), 1993, p 34.

We listen to these prophecies with openness and anticipation, longing for the day of fulfilment. In the renewal, God has opened our eyes to catch a glimpse of the possibilities.

Out of the mouths of babes . . .

We include here some of the children's stories, left in their own words, exactly as given to us, as we don't want to lose any of the simplicity of them in editing them.

A young boy, Cemlyn, aged 7 says:

> I was lying on the floor in a garden, it was thundering and lightning and I saw a sword come from the sky and hit me in between my arm and my body. Then I saw Jesus on a throne and a man dressed in black came in and attacked Jesus. Two men dressed in white came and took the black man away.

His sister, Angharad, age 9 shared this with us:

> I saw two angels and they were standing next to God's throne, one was beckoning to me, I think the one on the right. Then from behind them a voice said 'Come'. I felt like I was walking to the throne it seemed I had come a long way. Then God said 'Come, my child'. He appeared and the angels disappeared.

Our daughter Rebekah has seen other pictures besides the one mentioned earlier in this chapter. She says:

> I saw a green hill and a rainbow over it, at the top of the rainbow stood Jesus. Lots of people were going up the hill and trying to push past. Then Jesus said that it was no race as long as we got to the top in time.

When God showed Rebekah this picture she was lying on the floor and tossing her head and talking as in her sleep. We bent down to hear what she was saying. She said two words over and over again 'No race, no race, no race . . .' We looked at each other in bewilderment and it made no sense until she shared the picture with us. On another occasion as we were driving to Sunderland and she told us that she had 'butterflies in her stomach'. She was sure God was going to show her something that evening. During the time of worship Jane glanced at her and she was completely 'lost' in worship. Afterwards she told us what God had shown her during the worship time:

> I saw a room a little bigger than Sunderland but like Sunderland. It was full of people but I knew that they were angels because they kept disappearing and then coming back again.

Emma, a little 9 year old who is regularly at SCC, told us what God had done for her.

> I've been praying more recently, I pray that I won't get scared anymore and not have nightmares any more and he gave me a vision of a little girl who came up to me and told me God wanted me to be better and to be more lively.

Five more of these little children shared with us the visions that God had given them:
Cara (age 10):

> I saw angels . . . everyone was an angel . . . the room was full of angels, then God said he loved me and he'd always protect me.

Christopher (age 10):

> I saw lots of crosses and they started getting
> bigger, then I saw a big bright one.

Ellie (age 10):

> I saw a picture of a puzzle. All the pieces of it were all
> over the floor. I felt God saying that the pieces are
> the people and that when all the people get together
> it makes the church. Just like the picture needs all
> the pieces.
> I also had a picture of a bonfire and lots of sparks
> were flying off it. I think God was saying that the
> sparks won't just burn out but they will make big
> bonfires. The sparks which turn into bonfires is like
> starting new churches.

Sophie* (age 11):

> It was a picture of our school hall and it was all light.
> God was breaking through the stage. God also told
> me I'd work with children.

Victoria (age 11):

> I was in this white palace and I was walking with
> Jesus through it. He took me into a white hall. There
> was a throne and he told me to sit on it and he
> placed a crown on my head. It was magnificent.

Their little friend Jade who is just seven was with them.
When asked if God had spoken to her she replied:

> God just keeps saying to do things right.

We pray that as these little ones mature, the immediacy of God's presence remains with them.

CHAPTER 8

TEENS TALKING

Whilst God has been speaking to the little children, showing them simple truths about himself, he has been also doing some very deep things in the teenagers. We have seen with our own two boys and many of their friends just how profound the change has been.

Debbie is fifteen years old. We have often seen her at the renewal meetings, as she frequently helps with the stewarding and the music. She is a faithful and dependable young person. Whenever we see her we notice how she 'shines' with the love of God. Debbie shared her testimony with us.

'In these past few months of refreshing, God has really been dealing with me in many ways. As a young person he has changed my lifestyle. At one time it was as if I led two lives. It was friends some days and God other days, but now it is God every day. I still go out with my friends but it is different because they know I love God and I make sure that I don't get led astray with them.

'God has put this desire and a hunger and thirst in my heart for him. I have got a deeper love for him and I know his love for me is unconditional. I now know this not just in my head, but in my heart. I know that he will never let me down.

'I am unashamed to follow God. I feel free to worship

and open my heart to him and receive what he has got for me. I don't care what my family and friends think about me because I know I've got God. I have a heart for the lost and I believe that they will see God shining through the happiness I have got.

'Words cannot describe how I feel and I could talk about how much God has done forever. I did not think that as a young teenager I could feel this way over God, but I do, and I thank him for what he is doing. I have been healed of many things that happened to me as a child and God is setting me free. I feel that I was bound up in a chain and this chain is getting taken away from me link by link. It is taking time but it will be an ongoing thing, and God is going to break the chain and I will be completely free to follow him.'

From anorexia to God

Christie came to the refreshing meetings with a close friend in mid-November. She told us:

'What I thought was brilliant was that church seemed so different, everyone was happy and putting one hundred percent into the worship. During the ministry time I was really touched by the Lord and felt his presence . . . which I hadn't for a long time.'

Christie didn't return to the meetings for a few weeks. When she returned she knew that she needed a change in her life. She continues her story:

'I knew I didn't really love Jesus and I didn't love myself. As I lay on the floor I heard God telling me to go back to him. This was when I realised that my life was a huge mess. I had been anorexic, hated most of my family and was constantly dwelling on past hurts. It was then that I decided that God could have me. During the three months after this I have been changed in a drastic way.

'I won't do anything unless I know that God will agree. I now love God more than I ever have done and I know he loves me. I have been blessed so much that I can say I'm not really the person I once was. My friends at school have noticed a change and say I'm a much better person. There is nothing I would rather do than worship God— he is my real Father and will take care of me in all I do'.

Diane, also a fifteen year old, became a Christian when she was ten after seeing a miraculous change in the life of her parents. They had been 'saved' out of alcoholism and gambling. Diane is part of the local church at SCC, so has been in the renewal meetings from the start. She tells us how the refreshing has affected her:

'Over the last six months I've experienced so much love from God it's unbelievable. Church is no longer boring, but exciting and the best place to be. Jesus has become so real to me.

'I had a very low self esteem and I used to pull myself down quite a lot. God showed me how precious I was to him and I was not a mistake. Jesus took away all the rejection in my life and put love in my heart and gave me so much joy. He's put such a hunger in my heart.

'Over the weeks of the refreshing God has given me a desire to talk about him in school. I talked to four young girls about Jesus and they all decided they wanted to know him, so I prayed for them in school.

'Jesus is the best thing I've ever done. He is always there for me and I want to give him all the praise and just say thank you Jesus.'

Michael visited a renewal meeting with a youth group from his own church. He wasn't really interested but thought he might as well take the opportunity to see what was happening. Michael told us he enjoyed the service and for the first time in his life he fell down when he was prayed with. He went back to the meetings a number of times. He tells us his experiences of them:

'At first God went through my sins, one by one to sort them out. He brought up things that I'd never thought about. After that he started to bless me, much of it was to help me fight my sins.'

Then Michael had a picture, he described it for us:

'I felt I was in a boat. It had a sail and also oars. It was on a large river with God at one end and Satan at the other. There was a wind blowing from the good end to the evil end. This represented the world and its people. If I wasn't careful I would just follow the world and not God. To stop myself being swept towards Satan I had to continuously paddle. It's hard work to stand for Jesus, but it is worth it.

'I have been blessed and it's all helped me with my everyday life. I don't follow the crowd so much and my Christian confidence has grown immensely. I have found the whole time of blessing enjoyable and helpful and I hope it will continue.'

Passionate about God

Kate* is 18, and told us that, 'I can't imagine ever going back to the way I was as a Christian before this amazing time of refreshing.'

However, the last few months haven't been easy for Kate. God had to do a deep healing work in her.

'God's spirit was touching me right from the start, but it was a long journey. God had to release me from so much'. She continues: 'One night I fell in the Spirit and became very confused. God had brought things to the front of my mind. When I was younger my mum had gone to a fortune teller. This woman described the profession of the man who I would marry. I had forgotten about this but God released me from it that night.

'God continued to release me through the following months. I wanted to be completely free and to be blessed by God. One night I sat in my bedroom and just poured out my heart to God. Then the joy of the Lord fell upon me and I lay on the floor shouting, singing and praising God for over an hour.

'I am so much aware of God's presence and his amazing love for me. I have never felt so passionate about God and the depth of his grace has completely overwhelmed me. I used to find reading the Bible a chore, but now I can't seem to put the book down. God has opened my eyes to the Scriptures and I'm able to understand them in a new way.'

Gemma and Robbie are brother and sister from Hexham, Northumberland and worship at the Community Church there. Both are frequent visitors to Sunderland.

Robbie is the younger of the two. During the refreshing meetings Robbie was challenged about his lifestyle, particularly some of the music he had previously enjoyed. He feels that God has also set him free from embarrassment and self-consciousness. He remembers especially one of his first visits to Sunderland:

'Ken called all of the young people under twenty-five [years] out to the front. God put me out and, while I was down, I felt God telling me that I am going to be an evangelist.'

His sixteen-year-old sister feels God has changed a number of things in her life:

'I think the first major difference is the love for him that he has given me.

'Another major thing is that he has taken away the fear. I would go forward for ministry but as soon as anything started to happen I would tense up and back away from God. I realise how gentle God is and how he would never force me to do anything I didn't want to do.

'One thing that never ceases to amaze me is that feeling of peace that God gives me. Often he shows me things that I need to change and through his love I am changing them step by step.

'Throughout this move I just can't stop saying "thank you" to Jesus for what he is doing in me. I am so grateful.'

Fiona is another young lady who feels God is changing her. She feels that in the last six months her faith has really matured. Prior to the refreshing Fiona struggled with a lot of things in her life:

'He's given me strength to do things I couldn't have done before or by myself, including strength and help to give up smoking. I've also stopped going on drinking binges as God has shown me there's no point and I only get hurt and into trouble.

'I still accept that I'm a sinner, but now I try to live more godly in my actions and attitudes. The people around me have seen a change in me over the past months. Although it's been slow it's been steady and over time I've come a long way. God's still working in me and is totally in control of my life. I thank him for all he's doing and will do.'

Paul is a young man of fifteen who God is using greatly. Paul has been very powerfully gifted in prophecy and had visions which he has shared with the church. He has also been more able to witness at school. He recognises his increased love and desire for the things of God:

'I have a love for God bigger than ever before. I have a hunger for the Holy Spirit and just recently I have been set on fire for God. I have a much better relationship with

God than I did before the renewal came to SCC. I am willing to be used by him. People are noting a change in me, I have more love for people, and I am a lot happier.'

New boldness for God

The last stories from teenagers we wish to share are those of our own two teenage sons. We always think that it was sovereign of the Lord that we all came into the refreshing on the same evening in spite of the fact we were in different venues. Our youngest son, Ben, who is fifteen, reflects on his experience:

'I was standing in the long line, outside the 'big tent' at Harvest Camp '94, nervously awaiting the evening worship meeting. There was an excited buzz passing through the four hundred teenagers waiting to get into the marquee. I was waiting, hoping that what had happened last night would happen again tonight. I wasn't sure what it was but I was still anxious to get more.

'The previous night had been ecstatic. It was a usual teenage praise meeting. Lively music played loudly by Noel Richards and his band, humorous drama sketches, etc. The sermon that night was particularly good, even though I can't remember what it was about. What I can remember was the speaker, Jeff Lucas, giving an altar call to receive the Holy Spirit. I was sitting on the third row and I literally jumped over the two rows in front of me, clumsily knocking the people who were sitting near me. I hadn't a clue what I was expecting.

'The leaders began moving around praying for people, and to my surprise (and probably the leaders too) people began falling in the Spirit. I had seen people do this before, being the son of a charismatic Baptist minister, but never to this extent. By the time someone came to pray for me, which could only have been five minutes later, there were at least one hundred teenagers lying on the grass at the front and in the aisles. Others were laughing hysterically or crying. I got prayed for but did not go down, but instead joined the happy lot. I stood in this draughty tent in County Durham at 10.30 pm laughing. I got prayed for again and this time began swaying and found myself on the floor, now with about two hundred teenagers.

'Then, on September 3rd 1994, I was waiting to go into the tent again. On that day my parents had come to visit me and my brother. However, it was not new to them. The night before, when the blessing had fallen at this camp, they had driven for an hour to find Sunderland Christian Centre. The same thing had been happening there.

'The queue began moving and we crowded into the tent. We were not disappointed. God came again.'

That Sunday the whole family visited Sunderland. Ben tells us of his first impressions:

'We arrived at Sunderland and began winding our way through the city centre until we came to a poorer area. We turned up a road which was surrounded with a concrete jungle of high flats, many of them with their windows smashed. It was then that I spotted the church. It was a large clean building surrounded by a high iron fence. We arrived at the gates and were greeted by paid security guards and a large, savage looking German Shepherd dog. We were instructed to park on a patch of grass where we were hemming in other cars. The car parking spaces were all full, the road to get to these spaces was full and many other pieces of grass were parked on. More cars were coming in through the gates. I was amazed. There was still ten minutes to go until the service.

'We walked into the church and sat at the far left hand side. There must have been six hundred people here. I could hardly see the stage. The service started late and, immediately, Dad started behaving strange. He was trying to dance and kept bumping into me and smiling.

'The worship finished and a man stood up to give the announcements. He had black hair and a moustache. His name was Ken Gott. He began speaking with a Geordie accent but soon was forced to stop, being unable to speak a sentence which made much sense, because of laughter and a "mushy mind". A collection was then taken and then a lady with short blond hair began interviewing people about what God had done in their lives. I later found out that she was Ken's wife, Lois.

'People were doing things in this service which I had not seen before at Harvest. People were bending over and others were falling over without being prayed for. Ken was lying on the stage with both his legs in the air. He was making strange noises. This was certainly the strangest church service I had ever been in. In the past the preachers had always been able to sustain balance.

'After the service another strange order was given. We were asked to move all the chairs to the side of the hall. I couldn't figure out why they would clear up the chairs just to put them out again the next night. I soon found out. People began to get prayed for by the 'ministry team' who, Ken had assured us, were no better than any of us. The church soon looked like a battlefield with bodies all over the floor. I got prayed for and this time fell down straight away. It was a great start to a new school year. We got home after mid-night.'

However as we continued to visit SCC Ben started to notice a difference in his life:

'As I got prayed with more and more I began to manifest different things. I began "jerking" slightly and always twitched whilst on the floor. Not only were physical things happening to me, I was also changing inside.

Before God started blessing me I was always a bit nervous to talk to people about God. If people asked me questions I would try and answer them as quickly as possible and then talk about something else. I now found myself voluntarily telling people about Jesus. I always had an answer for their questions and I started quoting Bible verses I can't even remember reading.

'More recently I have got less shy in church. I have begun raising my hand and really worshipping God. This makes a difference - God is dealing with me much more deeply and I am manifesting more. Also at school I am happier. One day four different people told me I was happier. The more I worship God, and tell him I'm open, the more he fills me.'

Our eldest son, James, has also been touched in the present move of God. He likes to go to Sunderland as often as possible and is committed to serving on the ministry team three times a week. He tells us now how he feels the renewal has affected him,

'I have been going to SCC for about eight months, each time I go it seems to get better. It has changed me from the kid at the back of the room to the warrior at the front of the battle line. By this I mean that I feel on fire for God right now, more than ever before. Instead of like saying, "Oh no six more days till church". I now think 'Great it's time to go to SCC."

'Now I'm learning that this isn't just for meetings in a church building, but that it's going out into the city streets, and when that day comes I'll be ready. In all of this though I think that the thing that has happened most is my love for God has deepened.'

CHAPTER 9

LET MARRIAGE BE HELD IN HONOUR

We believe that marriage and the family, as Christians have traditionally understood it, is close to God's heart. The fracturing of family life, with its accompanying disruption and pain, tragically characterise much of our society. It has been good to realise that in God's renewing grace, marriages are healed and strengthened and families have found a new closeness to God as parents and children have been blessed together.

Jump in the puddles of God's love

The way whole families have been touched by God has been one of the most pleasing fruits of the renewal at Sunderland. It has for many not been merely an individual affair but an adventure which has healed and enriched marriages and given parents and children a new sense of togetherness in God. Anne told us:

'God has been changing our family during the refreshing, not so much in a dramatic way but gradually. I have been having a quiet revolution, and a revelation of the reality of God. God has been speaking and softening my heart, leading me step by step closer to him, until coming to a place of having my foundation totally on God himself and nowhere else.

'God's love is revealed (a new dimension); my past is revealed (a new perspective); my place is revealed (to belong only to him and sit at his feet); my heart is renewed (in love and responsiveness to God and to the family of God: to those who don't know God, and to his word.)'

Anne and David have five children aged between six and twelve years old. They have found their children very keen to attend meetings. Their eldest daughter went through a period of 'standing back', but after Anne talked it through, encouraging her daughter to talk honestly with God and to maintain her own integrity, she regained her spiritual hunger. Indeed, all the children speak of being closer to God since the refreshing. Two of the boys heard God speaking to them in different ways but clearly about God always being with them. One expressed it as a little boy walking with his mother on a rainy day and jumping in the puddles. 'God wants us to jump in the puddles of his love,' he told Anne.

Though externally Anne admits to no dramatic changes, she has noticed a definite increase in lovingness in the family: a greater desire to please God, and a new sensitivity in responding to God.

I wish someone would give me a hug

Bruce and Sandra testified to God doing a wonderful work in their marriage. Bruce, a dentist and Christian for 22 years, like many men in our culture, found it difficult to express any kind of emotions. Having been hurt in relationship with others, Bruce admits that he had 'made a decision to eradicate emotion from my life'. Even as a believer, though he knew that there had been a change on the inside, he found it impossible to show others what he felt. Externally, he tried to keep people, including Sandra, at a distance. Sandra admits that she had tried for twenty years to help Bruce move towards a greater emotional freedom and personal integration. Looking back on his experience in the renewal Bruce says, 'What Sandra failed to do in twenty years, God did in twenty seconds!'

In August 1994 Bruce and Sandra attended one meeting at the Airport Vineyard while on holiday (Bruce is a Canadian). On their return to the UK they immersed themselves in the renewal meetings, both at Sunderland and in their home church. Bruce expresses what happened during that time:

'In the first couple of weeks in September I would go to the (renewal) meetings. Before the meetings started I would be looking all around at the hall and at the people—looking and looking and looking. One night Sandra said to me "Who are you looking for?"'

Bruce was surprised by the answer he inwardly gave:

'I wish someone would give me a hug.'

Bruce had described himself as a 'machine living by logic', and he dismissed the thought quite easily. The next meeting Bruce was given a vision whilst resting on the floor in God's presence.

'I was lying on the floor and God walked up to me. I sat up and said to God that I needed a hug. He said back to me, "I want one too". We threw our arms around each other and hugged and hugged and hugged each other.'

Bruce eventually got up, found his two boys and gave them each a big hug. They found it all a bit embarrassing, but Bruce told them it was for all the hugs they had missed over the years.

The whole experience changed Bruce's view of God. He perceived that his relationship with Father God had been based on fear and not love: concerned with rules and regulations rather than a father-son relationship. He discovered that the God of the Old and New Testaments was the same God— a loving Father.

Bruce also found that people no longer kept him at arm's length. Where he had hated giving or receiving brotherly-sisterly hugs, now there were dozens. He says:

'This hug is really the love of the heavenly Father, to receive and give out. I keep having people come up to me and say how much I have changed. But I do not feel it as much as they say. I just feel I have a long way to go before the love that the Father has for the Son is in me. But I am going to keep on seeking my heavenly Father for more of his hugs and more of the Holy Spirit in order that I can show his love in my relationship to others.'

My family didn't need me

Frank loves people. He loves to pray for them, to encourage them and to share God's love with them. Diligently, Frank seeks out members of the ministry team to ensure that they too receive from God as well as 'giving out'. For Frank this has been a major turning around. Before the renewal he had become a broken, bitter and unpleasant man.

At fifty-three he was made redundant from his job as a chartered surveyor and became unemployed for the first time. At the time he didn't feel that his church helped and Frank withdrew into himself. He says:

'I continued to attend the church, believing that this was where God had placed my family, but every moment was personal agony. I avoided speaking to people, and when I did speak it was to criticise just about everything that the church was doing. Every leader was utterly wrong, every activity was entirely human, every person was living a lie!'

Outwardly, things were difficult. Inwardly, Frank was hurting deeply. He quite simply felt abandoned.

'I had seen that the world didn't need me—and even didn't want me. I felt that the church equally didn't need me and didn't want me. And I decided also that my family, now grown up, certainly didn't need me any more. Juliet was married and had a home of her own; Richard was making a successful career as a Naval Officer and Michael was sixteen taking his GCSEs. Grace would certainly be better off without me. So I concluded, as my family didn't *need* me, I would ensure that they also didn't *want* me.

'I took pains to withdraw myself from any family love and care. If an opportunity came to hurt them, then I took it. I did everything I could to drive them away. In that way I could prove my utter worthlessness to everyone, and I would have succeeded in something—however negative!'

Then came the renewal. Frank was a reluctant visitor using different excuses to both himself and Grace, his wife. But on his first visit it was the tender care of a retired senior pastor which seemed to reach Frank. Someone did care! Frank cried 'buckets of tears' that day as ministry team and Frank's own family prayed for him. Frank agreed to go to the next evening renewal meeting. He continues his story:

'During the ministry time, for the first time in my life, the unbending, dignified Frank lay on the floor for a long time. There were no blinding lights, no great words, no visions, just a sense of God's peace and presence.

'In the ensuing days God continued to meet with me on the carpet in Sunderland, and healed relationships which had been damaged or broken during the preceding months. People with whom I had difficulties, even unknown to them, would be alongside me on the carpet, seeking the same blessing.'

One time of ministry stands out as very important. As Frank lay in God's presence he heard an inner voice,

'This is my beloved son'. Frank thought immediately about Jesus. But the inner voice returned 'No, not Jesus, *you!*'

'I then saw this picture of me, being led by the hand past a crowd, whom I did not know, and the voice said to the crowd, "*This* is my beloved son." '

Through God's dealing with him, particularly the revelation of how much God loved him, Frank became a changed person. The barriers he had erected between himself, his wife and family were broken down. There was a precious family restoration through the love of God.

Renewal in English, Welsh, Russian, French . . .

Anne speaks four languages: her husband, Alwyn, two. We have heard Anne prophesy fluently in Russian when the Spirit of God has powerfully touched her! With their four children, they are one of a number of families who who have been deeply blessed together.

'The Lord has really swept through the whole family in a way we have never known before. The kids have amazed us with the sheer depth of what they have experienced— very often beyond their years. They have seen visions on several occasions and both boys separately said the Lord gave them swords to do battle with.

'The first time Gareth asked for prayer we were amazed because he has never shown any interest before. He was on the floor for ages and his dad had to carry him home because he couldn't walk. He then asked us if he was saved, said a prayer of commitment and asked for baptism. We were absolutely lost for words to see the Lord moving like that.

'Ellen has matured in her faith and knows the Lord in a way she never did before. She has become a real witness at school and seems to be developing a real care for the lost.

'The two little ones are so secure in their faith it amazes us. They both chat to friends and teachers openly about what is happening. Our major problem is the floods of tears and protests from them if they cannot get to church for some reason. They are still our kids, still squabble at times and still love the rough and tumble— but so changed! We can't explain it all to them, but then they never were much satisfied with our explanations of anything to them!

'The Lord has certainly been changing the grown-ups too. We are both conscious of a much greater love for Jesus, a much deeper prayer life together and the love of being with our own church family has increased.

'It's hard to highlight special occasions because we have had so many in such a short time—perhaps the morning Alwyn spoke to the Lord in Welsh from the floor for over half an hour, or the day a very respectable teacher was so drunk after church she had to be carried to the car . . .

'We have both known painful episodes when the Lord really dealt with long-standing problems and hurts. We had both given up thinking the Lord would ever use us again after several very difficult years full of hurt and rejection, but we were wrong about that. His plans are so obviously better than ours and the love he has for us far exceeds what we had deserved. There is still so much more!'

Love renewed

Sometimes when there are strange outward manifestations during the renewal meetings, the person affected is interviewed to discover what is going on. We have been anxious to root the outer, sometimes bizarre, appearance in the inner fruit of the Spirit.

We caught sight of Matt as he was struggling towards

the door. His body looked for all the world like it was made of rubber: arms, legs, torso, head all moving in strange uncoordinated ways yet propelling him out of the room. When he returned Matt was asked to come forward to be interviewed. What possible reason could there be for such odd behaviour in good company?

Those who were present were simply bowled over by what Matt told us. Matt and Milly had met later in life, fell in love and were married (both having been married previously). Sadly, their marriage did not work. Matt soon fell into ill health, nothing seemed to go right and after only two years they were divorced. Matt admits that he prayed that they might get back together but the horizon seemed bleak.

In October Milly attended the renewal meetings at Sunderland. She was given a vision by God which revealed to her that there was a large amount of unresolved anger deep inside her. He told her that she was to make an approach to her first husband (who had left her for another woman), seek forgiveness and then seek out Matt.

When she did so, they were reconciled and fell in love in a deeper way than before. Milly said, as she stood next to Matt, 'I just love him to bits.'

They wondered about remarriage, but Matt faced an unpaid bill for a large amount and it presented a dark cloud to them. They decided to pray. If they were to remarry somehow the debt needed to be paid. Soon afterwards a registered letter arrived for Matt. Some years before he had made an investment which he had forgotten about. It came at just the right time! As we write we are just two weeks away from their wedding day.

Listening to these two dear people speak, all of us were struck with the awesomeness of God. We freely admit that sometimes the outward manifestations in people's lives, as they respond to the presence of the Spirit, are difficult to understand. But we have seen again and again such wonderful fruit.

Running for God

Brian's is a similar story. We first saw him as he came to the front of a meeting to prophesy. Clearly the Holy Spirit was resting on him. As he came to the end of his brief prophecy, and a prayer was said for him, Brian took off running around the building. He ran around several times before falling to the floor.

Some weeks later, in a larger gathering during a conference, as the Spirit rested on him Brian took off again! Jane wanted to know what was going on inside Brian and she spoke to him at length after the meeting. Subsequently, he wrote his testimony in full. Again we were truly astounded by the way God moves.

Brian had been a believer for many years. Sadly, in 1993 he committed adultery with the wife of his closest friend. In God's goodness, the affair did not break up the families—good sense prevailed and the affair was ended. To make everything right both couples decided to see their church leader, to confess their sins, for there to be restoration in God and to have a new start. The result was not what they had hoped for. Rather than restoration there followed condemnation and lack of understanding from even close friends. Both couples left the church and went in separate directions.

Brian suffered severe depression feeling totally hopeless, realising that he had made a prison for himself. Brian admits that he 'struggled through 1994 with a lot of guilt, anger, resentment, self-pitying and shame, along with a sense of failure and loss of self respect.' In the meantime his wife, Teresa, found fellowship again in an open and accepting church.

God will use any and all means, at different times, to speak to his hurting children. Brian found himself watching the movie 'Forrest Gump' when God clearly addressed him. At a certain point in the film a young girl who had suffered abuse throws everything she can lay her hand to, in anger at that which had happened to her. When she finishes Forrest Gump remarks, 'There comes a time when there are no more stones left to throw.' God revealed the truth of that to Brian's heart. While everyone else in the cinema laughed, Brian sobbed his heart out. It was the beginning of his healing.

It was shortly afterwards that Brian heard of the renewal which had begun to touch the church Teresa had by now made her own. Brian attended meetings and God's healing continued. They also made the trip to Sunderland. Brian told us:

'A week or so before we went to Sunderland, I was by myself at one of the mid-week meetings . . . (Teresa and I call them "wobbly nights" as everyone wobbles and falls about!). I felt my legs starting to shake and then begin to move as though I was running. The next thing I know is I'm sprinting full speed around the auditorium. These words came to me, "Nothing will stop the march of the Lord across the land" and "You will run and not be weary."'

A similar anointing came upon Brian in the Sunderland meeting. When Brian responded to God he was already shaking more violently than he had ever before. He says, "I lay there for what I thought was only a few minutes. But it turned out to be three-quarters of an hour."

Through all of this God continued to heal Brian. The next night at Sunderland he was again deeply touched. It was at this meeting we saw him running for the first time. The wonder of it is that, in his own words, 'If anyone has seen me, they will say that I am in no way a runner. I'm 46, 2 stone (at least) overweight, little bow legs, and arthritis in my left knee to the degree of having to take six tablets a day and wearing a knee support.'

In the renewal God has touched Brian in other amazing ways which we have no space to tell. In one meeting he felt God saying, 'My people have been an adulterous people for too long. I am calling them back before it's too late. Return to the Lord now and rest in his blessing and not his anger.'

In a very real way Brian has lived that message and wants to share it with all God's people. There is healing, restoration and forgiveness issuing in praise to God.

The epilogue? On Sunday, April 2nd 1995 Brian and Teresa renewed their wedding vows before 200 people at their home church.

A family restored

By the summer of 1994 George*, Sue* and their three children Stuart*, Karl* and Katie* had been experiencing a difficult time. Their marriage had seen better times and their two sons were both experiencing difficulties at school and home.

Sue was first in the family to enter God's new blessing. As she was prayed for by a close friend and counsellor who had herself experienced renewal, Sue says:

'The power of God came upon me. Unable to stand I fell down as "electricity" coursed through me and my face burned and burned and my limbs did strange things. One second I'd be howling with mirth and the next with tears. This went on and on until I felt I could hardly take any more.'

The change for Sue was immediate and dramatic. When George joined her the following day he 'kept looking at [Sue] strangely'. He agreed to go that night to Sunderland and find out for himself what had happened to her. Sue reports:

'After these events George and I discovered we had changed. There was complete healing and forgiveness for the hurts between us and we felt closer than we ever had. We both found a new hunger for reading the Bible and for praying. George and I were both touched powerfully in the San Francisco Vineyard Church, whilst on holiday, where we received further healing from long standing hurts.'

Their three children were also deeply affected by the renewal. Karl had been experiencing problems at school. He couldn't seem to concentrate and caused problems for the other children and his teacher. So much so that an appointment was made to see an educational psychologist. However, before that happened Sue and Karl talked at length about Jesus and all that was happening. Karl gave his life to Christ. Again the change was immediate and far-reaching. Karl's behaviour at school altered dramatically. At a parents' evening the teacher, once exasperated by Karl, now congratulated Sue! Sue in her turn shared with the teacher the reality of Jesus and how it was he who had made such a difference to Karl. By the time of the appointment with the psychologist, Karl had changed such that the professional could find no reason for the interview!

George and Sue's eldest child had also experienced behaviour problems, but of a more protracted nature. However, Stuart having been touched by the Spirit in renewal meetings is a changed boy. Sue comments:

'He seems much "lighter" in himself, more cheerful in disposition and is very open to the things of God. He has become more tolerant towards his younger brother, much more kind.'

Even little Katie asked the Lord into her life and now talks about him to her friends at school. Her best friend Sarah had always been frightened of Karl. When Karl changed, Sarah simply couldn't believe it. Karl wanted to be friends—Sarah couldn't trust him, based on past experience. Sue prayed with Karl and Katie that Sarah would be able to see that Jesus had changed Karl. The next day at school home-time, Karl ran up to Sue saying incredulously, 'Guess what—Sarah loves me!' From then on all three children played together naturally.

A whole family turned around for God! Sue says:

'We give glory and praise to God for all these things. Without him we would be in a terrible mess and going nowhere. The fruit of the [renewal] for us has been reconciliation, forgiveness, peace, restoration of relationships, a whole new faith and trust in Jesus Christ and a new awareness of his immeasurable love for us and everyone. This is just the beginning.'

CHAPTER 10

SALVATION HAS COME TO THIS HOUSE

> It is strange, yet all too often true, that when the Spirit of
> God is working in supernatural power in revival, unbe-
> lievers will often be more quickly convinced that this
> work is wrought of God than some believers. . . [some
> believers] would have revival, but only if it comes along
> the quiet orderly lines of their own preconceived ideas.
> Where it is otherwise they will attribute the work to the
> flesh, or where this does not provide adequate explana-
> tion, to the devil.[1]

It has been said that the present renewal is a refreshing of
the church in preparation for revival. If that is true, then
we are not as yet in the period of harvest when great
numbers will be saved. Nevertheless, perhaps almost as a
by-product, as the people of God have sought his face,
when unbelievers have attended and seen the power of
God, often they make a commitment to Christ.

Between August 1994 and Easter 1995, the pastoral
team at Sunderland Christian Centre have documented
45 conversions to Christ relating to the local church at
Sunderland. That excludes any who have travelled to
Sunderland with friends from other churches, who have

[1] Arthur Wallis, *In the Day of Thy Power*, (Christian Literature Crusade:
Alresford, 1956).

made a commitment during the refreshing and have been discipled by churches other than SCC.

These conversions, we believe, point the way to God's heart for the near future of his church. Having revitalised the faith of his people, many who presently do not know him will seek his face.

We include here a few of those stories known to us.

A marriage made in heaven

'Now, tell us your name', Ken Gott said to the pretty, petite and radiant young woman who was about to be baptised. The young woman beamed as she replied 'Marie', then hesitated and proudly added her surname. The large congregation gathered to witness her confession of faith cheered loudly and clapped. 'And how long have you been Marie . . .?', prompted Ken. 'Since last Saturday,' came the reply.

Jim and Marie's wedding was the culmination of the most amazing few months in their lives. Jim had been at one time a nightclub bouncer and 1987 British Grand Prix bodybuilding champion. He was also no stranger to the seedier side of life in Sunderland and had spent time in prison for violent crimes. Marie had been his live-in girlfriend who had found her way to the renewal meetings at SCC. Impressed and deeply touched by the power and love of God she invited Jim to join her.

Eventually Jim came, bringing with him his young son, and was somewhat sceptical. Jim 'figured' that having such a large crowd each night with a collection taken every meeting someone must be on to a good thing! Jim didn't last too long that first night and literally ran out of the building. But something had certainly already happened to him: the Holy Spirit was beginning his work of grace. Besides, Jim had seen a wonderful change in Marie. Two

nights later he was back laying down a challenge to God
that there was just this one night for God to prove himself.

Jim made it through the meeting and during the
invitation, after the preaching, found himself walking to
the front, not to respond to God, but to tell the preacher a
few home truths. The worship and ministry had touched
him, but there was still much to sort out. The unsus-
pecting ministry team prayed for Jim as for any other
respondent. Jim fell to the ground enveloped in the power
of God. When he rose to his feet he was saved.

At this point, not even knowing right from wrong, Jim
had much to learn, but in the intensity of the renewal Jim
has developed a depth and maturity in a short time. He
heard God speaking to him about that which he had
gained from illegal activities and about Marie. He
realised that living together before marriage was not
God's best for them. Both had to be given up.

In the following months all involved in the renewal
came to love and respect Jim and Marie greatly. We saw
them both grow in their faith and have a deeply profound
effect on those around them. The love of God evidently
changing their lives is radiant upon their faces and in
their eyes. Jim has a heart to reach young people and is
now actively involved in helping them not make the same
mistakes he had made in his past life.

Jim and Marie are wonderful first-fruits, we believe, of
the coming revival.

Catching up fast!

We had seen Brendon a number of times at SCC. His was
one of those radiant faces shining with a light which we
have learned to recognise as of God. We had heard him
testify before, but on this occasion Brendon was 'beside
himself'. Even before Lois Gott reached him, to ask him

to testify, Brendon had begun to jog gently on the spot. By the time he spoke his gentle jog had turned to a trot. We had seen the Spirit of God fall upon people many times and from the sheer energy of his words (not to mention the outward physical manifestation) we were sure God was anointing Brendon powerfully. Even after he had shared Brendon continued to jog. In fact he ran out of the building for some time, to return later, and ended up running on the spot for the next two and a half hours. As we were leaving the meeting after eleven, somewhat tired having ministered to many, Brendon was still there, beaming the love of Christ and still running on the spot. Having learnt that the outward manifestations which happen to people are often, in some sense, a sign of the inner grace and revelation which God is bringing, we asked Brendon if he knew what God was doing. Though somewhat bizarre to those watching Brendon was aware of God's clear speaking.

'Brendon, you are running because you have a lot of catching up to do. I am going to help you catch up.' The outward and physical were God's sign to help Brendon understand a spiritual reality. To use a metaphor from Joel, God was about to restore to Brendon the years that the locusts had eaten.

So far, it has proved to be overwhelmingly true. Brendon's is one of the many remarkable testimonies to new life in Christ which have arisen out of the refreshing.

In his own words, Brendon lived in nightclubs 'trying to be a person I felt inside was not really me'. His life revolved around 'blonde girls, long legs, drink, fast food, fast cars, fast girls.' His recklessness led to a drink-driving charge, a hefty fine, the loss of his job as a sales representative with a nice salary and company car, together with a community service order.

It was then that God stepped into Brendon's life. The

whole turnaround in his life made Brendon search for some deeper meaning. God revealed himself and Brendon has not looked back.

His community service was to teach young lads, mostly from deprived backgrounds, how to play better football. Brendon had taught football coaching for eight years and his experience was put to good use. At first God gave him a great sense of love for the lads he was coaching. Then through a vision God directed Brendon to share the love of Jesus more directly with them. One night during ministry time at SCC Brendon saw a picture which made little sense to him. The picture was of markings on a field. Four days later God spoke to him:

'Brendon, it is half of a football field's markings. You're going to the kids, which is what I want you to do. But you're not telling them about me. You're only doing half of your job.'

Brendon became more open about his faith, asking God to help him share his love with the young footballers.

In these days of intense activity in God's Spirit this vision was only one of many experiences Brendon has shared. In his own words, 'Since I became a Christian I have had so many amazing experiences it would be impossible to be "of man". . . to put it into words—"awesome" wouldn't be enough.'

We relate one other of Brendon's stories. Having finished his community service at the YMCA Brendon has been taken on full time: an amazing testimony to God's goodness.

As part of his work Brendon met a friend whose daughter works for one of the major international sports and footwear manufacturers. Brendon came up with the idea of 'goody bags' for his young lads. His friend's response was something like 'no chance!'. Brendon persisted, eventually calling the daughter who, likewise, responded fairly negatively but said she would speak to her boss. An hour later she called back. 'How many would you like?' 'Of what?', Brendon replied. 'T-Shirts, caps, stickers and footballs.' Brendon placed his order for twenty! Then to his utter amazement, it transpired that his friend's daughter's boss was an old acquaintance with whom Brendon had played football ten years before. It made Brendon realise 'God's plan for me was at least ten years old!'

Found a family

We remember seeing Carol* on her first visit to SCC, that was in November 1994. She came with a friend of hers who had been to the church the previous spring for 'Sunday-at-Six' (these were a series of evangelistic meetings based on the Willow Creek model of 'seeker services'). Carol was not a Christian, but was happy to accompany her friend. Neither were aware of what had been happening since the summer . . . and so they walked into a refreshing meeting. Carol thoroughly enjoyed the meeting. She says:

'When I walked through the door it was like I left all my cares and woes at the door, it was so peaceful. I had often wondered if God existed. I was sexually abused by my father from being five until I was sixteen. If there was a God why was he letting me grow up like this?'

Carol went on to tell us that she had grown up with four sisters, yet they had never been a family. In the meeting she felt that sense of family. She describes it as 'such a lovely feeling'. After the meeting she went upstairs to get a cup of tea and to think about what she had heard and seen, but felt an urgency to return immediately to the meeting room. She went and stood in a corner and for the first time she spoke to God. She recalls:

'I said to the Lord, "If you want me, here I am". The

next thing I knew someone was praying with me and I hit the floor. I just lay on the floor. I said to God, "You can have me but I'm just a slab of concrete—a solid block of hatred." I didn't even like me. I've worked in a shop for ten and a half years and I'm always being told to be nicer, not to snarl at the customers. I used to think that I don't like people so why should I be nice to them.

'Since then (November '94) Jesus has turned my life upside down. He's given me a loving family of thousands and thousands and I know that he is always there no matter what. I remembered what happened to me as a child and burst into tears. He told me that none of it was my fault, I'd been carrying the guilt all these years, now I don't feel guilty.'

We had the privilege of seeing Carol get baptised in March at the same time as Marie. It was wonderful to see remaining fruit of the renewal.

Writhing with the love of God

We also had the privilege of being present at the meeting one evening at the end of March when Carl came forward in response to an invitation given for any who wished to commit their lives to Jesus. Carl is a young man in his late teens with sandy blonde hair and a winsome smile. When he talks about his recent decision he is radiant, shining with the love of Jesus.

He wrote his testimony for us and shared that he came to the meeting because he had decided he wanted to believe in God. He told us:

'I've just recently been released from prison after four years for attempted murder. Whilst in prison I noticed, one day, a Bible on the shelf and seeing as I was locked up by myself I decided to just have a quick look. I picked up the book and began to read. I couldn't believe it. Here I was, a drug dealer and attempted murderer, a man of bad ways, reading the Bible. I couldn't put it down, not only did I read it, but I read it three times.'

Carl went on to tell us that he also read a book by a man, Frank Constantine, who had become a Christian in prison. He also attended the prison church, but wouldn't let himself believe for fear of the other inmates and the loss of his tough image.

However, Carl was eventually released and a few weeks later came to SCC with a friend whom he had met at the hostel where he was living. His friend, Lee, had been greatly touched in the refreshing and still travels almost daily from Newcastle to Sunderland. Over the months a steady stream of other residents from the hostel have accompanied Lee as he has testified constantly to what God has done for him. Carl speaks of that first meeting:

'I was touched by the Holy Spirit and fell to the floor writhing with the love of God pouring all over me. Since God came into my life I have given up using drugs and even moved to a new city so that I can start afresh and be led by God instead of returning to crime. Before I found God I felt empty inside, I didn't realise this until I had found him. I didn't understand why God had sent the Spirit to touch me. I know now even sinners and people as bad as I was can be touched by God because of his powerfulness. From now on God will guide me and my life will be in his hands.'

My arm shot up in the air

Suzanne had always known about Jesus. Religion had been part of her upbringing. Even when she became severely ill she had assumed it was God's punishment for past deeds. However, after many months she started to recover. She says, 'It was then I realised how lucky I was to be alive. Life was back to normal. I started going back to mass on a Sunday.'

Suzanne was taken to a renewal meeting at Sunderland by a friend. 'I realised how much of a hypocrite I really was. I was totally taken aback by the way the Holy Spirit was showing his presence and working with his people. I realised for the first time in my life that the God I prayed to was really there.

'The pastor asked if there was anybody who wanted to become "born again". I had not given it much thought but before I knew what I was doing my arm shot up in the air.

'That same night I was born again, prayed for and I can only say the feeling I received was wonderful.'

This all happened just a few days ago. As we write, Suzanne told us how she has been feeling since then:

'My life has not changed dramatically. But I know that having felt the presence of the Holy Spirit in me and around me, there are going to be some changes in my life. I look forward to these.'

May there be many more like Jim, Marie, Brendon, Carol, Carl and Suzanne!

CHAPTER 11

WORDS OF WISDOM
AND EXPERIENCE

The Metrocentre on the outskirts of Gateshead is still, to
our knowledge, the largest out-of-town shopping complex
in Europe. We sat with our new friends Herbert and Mary
Harrison in one of the Centre's many restaurants and
cafeterias enjoying good fellowship and hot bacon
sandwiches. The four of us were reflecting on the previous
six months, hardly believing where the time had gone and
yet feeling we had known one another for years.

Herbert is a retired pastor of great wisdom and maturity who has reached his seventy-third year. He had
founded and successfully led the Bethshan Christian
Centre in Newcastle-upon-Tyne to be the largest church
in the North-East of England. The leadership of the
renewal is, for the most part, in the hands of those in their
thirties and forties (just). Having Herbert and Mary
around has provided something of a sense of security for
those of us who are younger. We know, of course, that our
security is in God, but having dear saints giving their
approval, who have been tried and tested in the furnace
again and again, has helped us a great deal. Many times
we have been at the very limit of our experience as God
has brought new things before us. It has been good to talk
with Herbert and Mary, to hear their experience, receive
their counsel and their prayers and to press on again.

Mary and Herbert have been in the renewal since the beginning (Lois Gott is their daughter!). We asked Herbert to write his reflections on the renewal at Sunderland. This is what he wrote.

'From time to time in a long pastorate of thirty-seven years one is faced with innovations and emphases that can be both challenging and disturbing.

'A movement arose in the fifties that brought a new liberty and freshness to worship. It was welcomed at the time when Pentecostals generally had settled down and had become victims of their own tradition. But it was discredited because it majored on a liberty that gave little time to sound teaching from the word of God.

'The life of the Spirit is vital to healthy growth, but it must never be at the expense of balanced ministry from the Scriptures. Donald Gee once remarked, "All word and no Spirit, we dry up. All Spirit and no word, we blow up. Word *and* Spirit, we grow up." '

'In the seventies the shepherding movement brought its own challenges and significance, aspects of which touching discipleship were sound and Bible based, but extremes in the area of authority and submission rang warning bells throughout the charismatic movement, resulting in much hurt and division.

'My own attitude to disputable innovations and emphases over the years has been one of caution, very much like Gamaliel's stand in Acts 5. Actually, cautious fence-sitting is not the ideal when fear is the motivating factor. Men and women who have moved mountains for God have been risk-takers.

'It *is* important that we "try" the spirits and prove all things (1 Jn 4:1, 1 Thess 5:21) to see whether they are from God. But having said that, it is vital that we do not come to a foreclosed judgement based on hearsay, and limit God to our restricted understanding of what is acceptable and what isn't. I made up my mind during the seventies that I wouldn't be a reactionary preacher. If the devil pushes some to extremes and the truth is hurt in the process I wouldn't react negatively and "throw out the baby with the bath water." It is Satan's ploy to get us to close our minds to things we don't fully understand.

'Since August 1994 I have been actively involved in the Sunderland experience. It has been deeply moving to witness a hunger for God in people committed to travelling over great distances for a single meeting, with many from the continent and further afield, joining them in seeking God for themselves.

'I felt uncomfortable at first with the variety of manifestations, remembering a time of renewal in Newcastle during the eighties when I ended abruptly a similar outbreak, judging it to be extreme and unscriptural. From that time our growth momentum slowed down perceptively. I wasn't going to make a similar judgement this time round. With R.T. Kendall, speaking in London, "I would rather handle electricity with wet hands than say that what is happening is of the devil." Of course there will be manifestations on the part of emotionally unstable people; there will be attention seeking exhibitionism, but it is gratifying to witness the correcting, regulating work of the Spirit going on. In one place, as ministry time began a responsible and Spirit-filled brother saw shadowy figures scampering away from individuals. What better place for demonic powers to be effectively dealt with than where the presence of God is powerfully manifested.

'Many ask, "What is behind the losing of strength and falling down, the laughing, the crying, the trembling etc?" I cannot answer that in total honesty, but what I can say with some conviction is that lives are enriched, parched and dried up believers quickened and renewed, embittered parties reconciled after years of not speaking, long-standing marriage problems healed, addictions broken, violent people converted and maturing in an astonishingly short time.

'I have to say that if what is happening is of the devil, as some have foolishly stated, he is not as bright as he is made out to be! He is working against himself, because the one outstanding characteristic coming out of all that is happening in Sunderland is the intensifying of personal love for Jesus Christ, and Jesus Christ, you must know, is the implacable enemy of the devil.

'When there is a work of God you can expect persecution. The Welsh revival in 1904 was rejected by some leading churchmen, so were the revivals under Charles Finney and Jonathan Edwards.

'I am asked occasionally if any of the physical manifestations have happened spontaneously to me and I have to answer "No", although I am open to such as far as I know how to be.

'I am under no pressure to receive such as evidence of God's acceptance of me, because my focus is not on what happens externally but on Jesus Christ and what he wants to do in me. "By their fruits you shall know them," Jesus said and the fruit of the Spirit is love, joy, peace, etc (Gal 5:22).

'I fully accept that God is sovereignly refreshing the church world-wide. It is an experience that must sooner or later break out into the Acts of the Apostles society-changing, city-shaking, men-women-and-children-converting experience. Anything that falls short of that will finish up as a protracted self-interested brand of Christianity unworthy of God. But I believe that already strong prophetic voices are pointing that way and we shall see an unprecedented gathering in of a world-wide harvest very soon.

'Let it come Lord.'

Herbert writes with the balanced wisdom of long years

in the pastorate, having experienced Christianity for more than half of this century and having passed through his own successes, and occasional failures.

Interview with John Arnott

On the Wednesday of the Easter conference (see Afterword) we had the privilege of having lunch with John Arnott. John has taken a particular interest in the renewal at Sunderland. He had earlier that day shared something of his story with the conference delegates, but we wanted to press a little further.

John Arnott is a large, warm, personable and endearing man . . . like everyone's favourite uncle really! It has been commented upon more than once in the Press that he bears an uncanny resemblance to the actor John Goodman (the screen husband of Roseanne and the inimitable Fred Flintstone in the movie). John and Carol have two sons (Carol's) and two daughters (John's); both were formerly married and divorced. Their youngest offspring is twenty-four, and the oldest thirty-two. They have four grandchildren. They married in 1979 when John, in his own words, had 'no concept of how lovely women were'. Carol literally 'loved me back to life'.

Even after a brief time in fellowship with him, John Arnott is the kind of person you feel you have known for a long time. We asked why it seemed that way. John answered:

'We try to be transparent. We have nothing to hide. The Lord prompts me gently to tell it like it is. It keeps you humble and God puts a high value on humility. Once you start pretending that you are successful, or you are something you are not . . . your own heart starts to tell you "come on" . . . I find it's just easier to tell everybody. It's astounding to me to come to England and have 3000 people turn up for a conference. That's never happened, but we are accepting now that God is using us to facilitate the renewal. I'm committed to seeing it furthered and continued in the same values that are important to me, in humility, with nobody marketing the thing and milking the thing and taking credit for the thing. The Lord told me initially that he did not want me to market this or to exploit the renewal to expand my own ministry. Rather to stay low and not to advertise it. I have to say that the Lord advertised this thing massively. We have hardly had a negative report in the secular Press.'

That statement, in itself, is quite remarkable and we asked why it might be. John believes it is because they have always been open with the Press and answered media interest with honesty and frankness.

We all have our personal heroes and we asked John who had impacted him personally. His answer: 'Billy Graham, Kathryn Kuhlman, Benny Hinn, Claudio Freidzon . . . [and] Randy Clark and I tended to spark each other. It just exploded.'

In a very short space of time John and Carol Arnott have been given an international reputation which is quite staggering. We wanted to know how the unexpected high profile had affected their lives and if there were any temptations with it. John replied:

'Mostly we are out of touch with it. . . [It's like] . . . "What do you mean international profile?" We just like hanging around with people like Ken [Gott]. We just say to pastors, "You don't need us. Just go home and do what we do." '

He continued, 'Well we've gone from being ordinary obscure Vineyard pastors to international visibility. You know it's the craziest thing. How are we to deal with that? We know who we are. We're still very ordinary. Neither of us are highly educated. I didn't even finish my degree. I dropped out about two months before graduation. . . The point is, if we can do it, anyone can. That needs to be said to encourage people. People describe us as being very loving. It flows from Carol originally, but the world is absolutely needing to see Christian churches that are loving, caring churches.'

Clearly, life has not always been smooth for the Arnotts. Having planted an independent church in Stratford, Ontario (Carol's home town) in the early 1980s, they saw a wonderful move of God. Sadly, after a good beginning it began to go astray. John comments, 'It went a bit weird'. John and Carol reacted by restricting all prayer for others in the meetings to themselves alone. Looking back John realises that 'We killed a move of the Spirit'. As a result they made a commitment to God that if, in his goodness, he moved powerfully again they would not restrict him. With many others around the world we're glad they made such a vow! It seems clear that their previous experience prepared them for the outpouring of the Spirit at the Airport Vineyard.

John is, however, the first to admit that they have not been able to meet everyone's needs. They do now, however, have a church full of people who share the same vision and goals.

Yet the renewal was not a total surprise to the Arnott's. There were no less than five prophecies given to them that the renewal was coming summed up by John as 'Basically, you're going to the moon for God!' Their response was simply, 'God, do what you want to do.' Though John admits that he wasn't holding his breath at the time!

We asked John where he thought the renewal was going.

'We have told the Lord that we will keep going as long as he sends people. The crowd goes down, the quality goes up. The quantity goes down, the quality goes up as you have more time to soak people. There will be anywhere from 1200 to 2000 every night in the meetings. We are worried about the summer as so many are coming. It's almost like we need to issue an international call. If you are on a ministry team and can furnish a pastor's reference, come and help us.'

We wondered, too, how the current renewal was perceived by John Wimber, who continues to lead the international Vineyard movement.

'He has been a great help and a great friend. He has always encouraged me to go for it. He loves the power of the Spirit.'

However, the present move of the Spirit is evidently different to that of the 1980s. 'John Wimber wasn't too thrilled at first about the idea of catchers. (Those who stand behind people who are prayed with.) The difference is the opportunity to soak people in prayer. If there is a general invitation, "Come Holy Spirit", it will hit about 10%. If you invite people forward individually you will get about 90%.'

John Wimber has been generally encouraged by the fruit of the renewal. John [Arnott] commented further on the Vineyard churches in the renewal.

'Because we were Vineyard, interest at first flowed through the Vineyard network. I certainly called my friends. Ninety per cent of Vineyards are doing the same as we are.'

The April conference was the second visit of the Arnott's to Sunderland, with a particularly special bonding being forged between the two 'wells' of the Spirit. We asked if John had any idea why Sunderland became like a smaller version of Toronto? He commented:

'We can only speculate. I know God uses people. Ken and Lois got powerfully touched. They had a desire to do it. They went back home. God exploded on them and they had the faith to keep it going. God is looking for people who are willing to pay the price, risk it all and go for it.'

There are many around the world who have taken that same challenge seriously. From our experience and observation we can honestly say that many of those involved in the renewal at Sunderland have found a new willingness to pay the price, to risk all and quite simply, to go for all that God is willing to give them. It has been a tremendous joy to share with so many who have such a heart for God.

AFTERWORD

Easter Conference 1995

We feel we can't end this book without including an account of the Sunderland conference with John and Carol Arnott from the Airport Vineyard. The conference took place on the 11th-13th April 1995 and provided a fitting climax to all that God had been doing through the Sunderland renewal between summer 1994 and Easter 1995.

In a time of testimony and sharing during the conference our good friend Robert Ward from Newcastle shared a word he believed God had given him. Robert is director of North East Area Revival Ministries and an ordained Anglican minister. He shared that he, like many others, had doubted that God could work powerfully in the North-East of England and urged repentance for any who had thought similarly. God had revealed to him that, 'The heart of the flame of the Spirit burns in the North-East with an intensity which is phenomenal'.

Robert's words found an echo in the hearts of all who attended the conference, which provided both a capstone to the previous eight months and a springboard for all that is to come. We believed that the renewal entered a new phase in which we were to see a greater intensity in the power and the love of God. It had been prophesied that a time was coming when we would see many come to know Jesus as Lord, together with powerful manifestations of the signs of the kingdom as recorded for us in Matthew 11: The blind see; the lame walk; lepers are cleansed; the deaf hear; the dead are raised; the wretched of the earth learn that God is on their side.

The conference took place in the Northumbria Centre in District 12 of Washington, which forms part of the city of Sunderland. Members of Sunderland Christian Centre worked hard to organise the mammoth event. A small army of volunteers worked tirelessly and ceaselessly during the three days. For many it meant being on the premises from very early morning until the early hours of the following day. The servant hearts of these dear sisters and brothers was testimony itself to all that God had done in the previous months.

Over 1,300 people had registered for the full three days with several hundred others enrolled as day visitors with the evening meetings being open celebration. Many had travelled hundreds of miles to attend. We know of people who had come from Holland, Norway, France, West Africa, New Zealand, Australia, Thailand as well as all over the British Isles (including Northern Ireland and the Orkneys). On the first day, as the afternoon session began drawing to a close and we left the building to get 'a breath of fresh air' and a moment's rest, we saw the first coach drive up full of people eager for the evening celebration!

Over the months we had spent many hours soaking in God's presence and yet during those three days we again felt and saw something different. It was as if we had 'changed gear'. Our two teenagers, along with many others, seemed to spend the whole time drunk in the Spirit. Many of the young people were filled with an even stronger desire to evangelise.

We saw people responding to God: many came forward for salvation: others came forward to receive prayer for broken marriages and relationships: yet others to receive prayer pertaining to different callings on their lives as evangelists, prophets, leaders and intercessors. The ministry team tirelessly prayed for all who wished to receive at the conclusion of each meeting: every night probably over a thousand people fell under the power of the Spirit and lay row after row, side by side as they soaked in God's presence.

First–fruits of healing

We saw people healed under the power of God as, we believe, a sign of that which is to come. Two in particular are worthy of note.

A young lady doctor had badly broken her arm ten days before the conference. Towards the conclusion of one of the meetings she ran to the front waving the cast from her arm in the air. She testified that during the meeting her arm had begun to shake within the cast. As the shaking increased in intensity the cast began to move until it was eventually shaken off. As it came off she realised that she had been healed. She flexed the fingers on her hand and realised immediately that a miracle had been performed. We were open-mouthed as she explained to us the medical nature of the fracture, and the exact bone which had been broken.

The following meeting Caroline, a nurse from an intensive therapy unit at a large Newcastle hospital, rushed to the front and started jumping up and down. She touched her toes again and again declaring that God had healed her. When the excitement subsided she managed to tell us that she had suffered from a degenerative back and foot condition and was becoming unable to work. We had seen her many times at Sunderland, using a stick to help her walk and to support herself when she stood. It was wonderful to see her healed and giving the glory to God. Interestingly, both women were from the medical profession and were able to testify to healing and give medical support to their previous condition. We believe these two stories are only a foretaste of what God has in store for his church as we move towards revival.

Final testimonies to God's goodness

Between the meetings we took comments from a few of those present. All seemed to have been really blessed by God. We include these as the comments of a completely random selection of people. We wandered over to speak to various groups whilst they were eating their sand-wiches! They shared with us how they felt and how God had touched them during the meetings.

'Feels like something opening inside your heart, it's the sense of the presence of God in your heart.' Trevor (Telford)

'It's like waves coming over you, gloriously intoxi-cated.' John (Liverpool)

'I'm burning, there's a fire in me starting from the inside going out, it's like I've been microwaved by the Spirit. God's also given me visions and I feel I've been called into youth leadership.' David (Carlisle)

'I know God loves me as an absolute concrete fact.' Rosie (Poynton)

'People we know are being radically altered from the roots.' Sarah and Lynn (Inverness)

'I've seen people's lives change who I knew before. Then I realised that the manifestations aren't that important, as their lives are being changed.' Caroline (age 15, Newcastle)

'I love the conference, I love the refreshing. I couldn't stop laughing and God is doing inside me things that match the outward manifestations. I love it when the Spirit comes down.' Noreen (Peterborough)

'Lovely gentleness and presence of God. Every meeting God has done something different which shows it is not manipulated.' John (Leeds)

'It's brilliant . . . it's fantastic that you can pray for the Lord to pour it (the Spirit) out and then he does.' Joan (Millfield)

'I was wondering why I was sat "like a stuffed dummy" feeling nothing when all around people were laughing. Then John [Arnott] said one third received like lightning rods, one third by feelings and one third by faith. Then I believed I was in the faith . . . I don't have to roll round to receive, so I really enjoyed it. It was worth taking my holidays for.' Eleanor (South Shields)

'It's been brilliant. We just know there is a real heavy presence of the Lord here, a real anointing.' Mandy and Shalane (Peterborough)

'It's very good, a great movement of the Holy Spirit. I was very surprised to see English people worshipping and praising the Lord so uninhibitedly. When I was sitting I saw that the Norwegian people have lost worshipping in many churches, I feel a burden on my heart to restore worshipping.

'I'm happy to see all different age-groups, the wall between age-groups has come down as a result of the refreshing. Also the wall between denominations, there is good spiritual unity. It is a good sign for revival and refreshing.

'When I heard about it two weeks ago I wanted to experience it and take the fire to Norway.' Gunnar Feppestol (Norway)

'It's the best time I've had in a long time. It just seemed to bring me, personally, new hope. Soon all teenagers and children will be able to see it and realise that there is hope for them.' Debbie (age 16 Liverpool)

'Warm, friendly atmosphere, powerful presence of the Lord. I've received a blessing, it's lovely to be here and drink it in. I can't wait for the next one.' Graham (Pontllanfraith)

'Just nice to see God move in his people, releasing and giving joy. God's given me the joy, so I know that it's real.' Diane (Leeds)

'We've never been to a conference like this. What has spoken to us most is the love of God, the heart relationship. People need to love each other, churches need to love each other and this will only spring from us receiving the love of God.' Betty and Geoffrey (Pickering)

'Wonderful to see so many people willing to take off all the restraints and say "Anything God, whatever you want."' Julie and Doug (Brighton)

'It's mind-blowing, awesome, so many hungry people. You feel like you are sitting and soaking in God's presence. Not even just in the meetings, but in between them, the atmosphere doesn't change.'
Faith and Sue (Manchester)

Sustaining renewal

Historically speaking, renewal movements are time-limited—the renewal lasts, sadly, only a matter of months or a few brief years at most. However, the impetus which such movements give to the church often issue in many new churches and creative initiatives in the kingdom of God.

We have been in renewal now (if January 1994 is counted as the beginning) for some fourteen months. At Sunderland we have known eight months of what Martyn Lloyd Jones called 'days of heaven on earth'. We have wondered how much longer will the renewal continue? Will the time of refreshing give way to days of national revival? Will the Christian church have a part to play in turning the Western liberal democracies away from their morally and spiritually disastrous course?

Perhaps behind all of our wondering has been the question of how to sustain renewal. We offer four concluding thoughts.

The sovereignty of God

In sustaining renewal we do need to be aware that the God we serve is sovereign in all his ways and works. He is not a 'pet' obediently obeying our calls to him—he remains sovereign Lord of the church. What we, and others all around the world, have experienced, can only be attributed to his sovereign mercy and grace. We are acutely aware that we have gathered where others have sown. The story will perhaps never be told of those dear saints of God who have interceded for an outpouring of the Holy Spirit on the church. We know of faithful ministries where good people have laboured for years and years seeing little fruit. And yet we have seen much. We don't boast about it, we thank God. Why he has chosen this generation, this particular time, the people and the churches around the world he has, we can give no answer to. From time to time God sovereignly pours out the Holy Spirit with great intensity. We are in such a time. Our prayers need to be continually of thankfulness and pleading with God that in his sovereign grace this time of renewal continues. We are utterly dependent on him.

The utter goodness of God

Yet his sovereignty is based upon his character, the personal attributes of God—the kind of being he is. It is here, quite possibly, that to sustain renewal we need something of a change of mind. Undoubtedly, for some of us, our understanding of God has been that in some ways he is capricious, unpredictable in a bad way, and often withholding his blessing to 'teach us a lesson' in some way or other. However, the Father as Jesus revealed him is not like that at all. God is full of goodness, full of love and delights in giving good things to his children. Luke expresses it most clearly:

> So I say to you, Ask, and it will be given you: search, and you will find: knock, and the door will be opened for you. For everyone who asks receives, and everyone who searches finds, and for everyone who knocks, the door will be opened. Is there anyone among you who, if your child asks for a fish, will give a snake instead of a fish? Or if the child asks for an egg, will give a scorpion? If you then, who are evil, know how to give good gifts to your children, how much more will the heavenly Father give the Holy Spirit to those who ask him!
>
> Luke 11:9-13

We have begun to realise that our Father *does* want to bless us in an overabundant way and that when we ask for his Spirit he delights to give it.

God's sovereignty is based upon his utter goodness and beneficence. When he is revealed as such to us then our faith expectation rises. We might, then, expect that God would bless his church in the way he has. Our prayers for the sustaining of the renewal are directed to a sovereign *and* good God.

Hungry and thirsty people

In a sermon preached about a month into the renewal at Sunderland, Ken Gott shared that he had asked God how long nightly renewal meetings were to continue. The answer Ken received was that renewal was to continue as long as there were vessels to be filled. Ken had been considering the story where Elisha helps the prophet's widow through the miracle of continuous oil. In the story the woman was to find as many vessels from her friends as she could. The miracle occurred in that as she poured from her small jar of oil into all the other vessels, the oil kept pouring. The story finishes, 'When the vessels were full, she said to her son, "Bring me another vessel." But he said to her, "There are no more." Then the oil stopped flowing (2 Kings 4:6).

It became something of a motif, for the renewal at Sunderland often referred to. As long as there were vessels to be filled the oil of the Holy Spirit would continually be poured out.

In sustaining renewal it is imperative that people are hungry and thirsty for God. Whenever people become blasé about the move of God, complacent about his goodness and gifts and lose their spiritual desperation and hunger, then renewal will stop. We have prayed many times, 'Lord, keep us hungry and thirsty for you.'

Open to God and willing

If hungry hearts and thirsty spirits are a prerequisite to sustaining renewal, then an openness and willingness to follow God wherever and in whatever way he desires is equally essential.

The likelihood is that when God 'arrives' it will be in a way which we are initially unprepared for. The 'packaging' of the prophets was a surprise to Israel, the birth of the Messiah in a stable and not a palace brought confusion to some, and opening the door to the Gentiles caused problems for many in the early church.

When God brings renewal it is often accompanied with that which might cause us to stumble. In virtually every renewal movement there have been those outward and visible manifestations which have caused people to question. Even those hungry and thirsty for God—they may have even been praying for God to visit his church—have pause for reflection: 'Am I really open to God and willing to be, do, go and receive anything that he wants for me?'

There will always be the risk of faith. Total certainty is reserved for 'glory' when we will know as we are fully known. For now, hungry and thirsty for God, we express our willingness to be led by him.

In the early summer of 1994, Andy received a word from God which came from Martin Luther (via Dietrich Bonhoeffer):

Discipleship is not limited to what you can comprehend—it must transcend all comprehension. Plunge into the deep waters beyond your own comprehension, and I will help you to comprehend even as I do.

Bewilderment is the true comprehension. Not to know where you are going is the true knowledge. My comprehension transcends yours. Thus Abraham went forth from his father and not knowing wither he went. He trusted himself to my knowledge, and cared not for his own, and thus he took the right road and came to his journey's end. Behold, that is the way of the cross. You cannot find it yourself, so you must let me lead you as though you were a blind man, no living creature, but I myself, who instruct you by my word and Spirit in the way you should go. Not the work which you choose, nor the suffering you devise, but the road which is clean contrary to all that you choose or contrive or desire—that is the road you must take. To that I call you and in that you must be my disciple. If you do that, there is the acceptable time and there your master is come.[1]

There is, undoubtedly, something of mystery and depth in those words. They do, however, point us in the direction of faith seeking God's way and not our own. They speak of willingness to be open to all that God has for us.

God willing, that is how we choose to be. Believing in a sovereign and good God, hungry and thirsty for more of him, we gladly and willingly open our hearts to all that he has for us.

Even so—more Lord!

---

[1] Martin Luther in Dietrich Bonhoeffer, *The Cost of Discipleship*, (SCM: 1948), pp 83–84.

APPENDIX

Books Documenting the Renewal in 1994-1995

Wallace Boulton, (ed). *The Impact of Toronto*. Monarch: Crowborough, 1995.
> A compilation of articles in Renewal magazine from a variety of authors.

Guy Chevreau. *Catch the Fire*. Kingsway: Eastbourne, 1994.
> Guy Chevreau teaches at the Airport Vineyard Toronto. There is particularly important historical theology relating to the Great Awakening in the eighteenth century.

Patrick Dixon. *Signs of Revival*. Kingsway: Eastbourne, 1994.
> Patrick Dixon's book is very insightful with regard to the physical manifestations associated with the renewal.

Andy and Jane Fitz-Gibbon. *The Kiss of Intimacy*. Monarch: Crowborough, 1995.
> This book relates to the fruit of the renewal in terms of intimacy with Christ.

Dave Roberts. *The Toronto Blessing*. Kingsway: Eastbourne, 1994.

Dave Roberts, editor of Alpha magazine, helpfully documents the renewal from the beginning in a very readable fashion.

Rob Warner. *Prepare for Revival*. Hodder and Stoughton: London, 1995.

Rob Warner gives a thoughtful and insightful theology of the renewal.

Andy and Jane Fitz-Gibbon
can be contacted at

In Christ Ministries
PO Box 27
Hexham
Northumberland
NE46 3RD

In Christ Ministries
PO Box 4973
Ithaca
NY 14852